Contents

1

First Things First

Y ou're probably sitting at your computer with the DOS prompt (C:\>) on your screen. More than likely, you have letters and reports to write, and you're anxious to get started with WordPerfect for Windows. But first, those of you who have never used WordPerfect for Windows before need to cover some basics, such as how to get around WordPerfect's document window, select parts of a document, give instructions, save and open documents, and back up files. In this chapter, we also review some Windows techniques, but we assume you've used Windows enough to be familiar with basic operations. (If you are new to Windows as well as new to WordPerfect for Windows, we suggest you read *A Quick Course in Windows*, another book in the Quick Course series.) After you learn a few fundamentals, you'll easily be able to create the documents we cover in the rest of the book.

If you are already familiar with WordPerfect 6 for Windows, this book brings you quickly up to speed with WordPerfect 6.1 for Windows. You can skim this chapter for information about new and improved features and then get down to work with Chapter 2.

Getting Started

We assume that you've already installed both Windows and WordPerfect 6.1 for Windows on your computer, and that you're ready to go. (We don't give detailed instructions for installing the program because WordPerfect guides you through the process.) We also assume you're using a mouse. Although it is possible to work with WordPerfect for Windows using only the keyboard, the Windows environment is tailor-made for point-and-click mouse techniques, and using a mouse with WordPerfect for Windows is both intuitive and efficient.

The simplest way to start WordPerfect for Windows is from the Windows Program Manager. Follow these steps:

1. Type *win* at the C:\> prompt, and press Enter.

2. If necessary, double-click the WPWin 6.1 group icon to open the WPWin 6.1 group window.

Clicking and double-clicking

Clicking is a simple matter of pressing and releasing the mouse button once. To double-click, you *quickly* click the mouse button twice. If double-clicking doesn't produce the anticipated result, try again, this time clicking a little faster.

WordPerfect

3. In the group window, double-click the WordPerfect icon to start the program. WordPerfect's copyright screen makes a brief appearance, and a few seconds later, you see this document window:

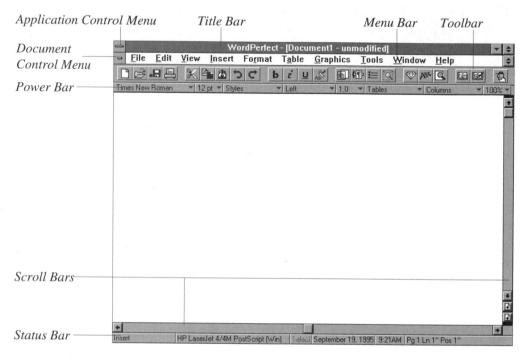

Application Control Menu *Title Bar* *Menu Bar* *Toolbar*

Document Control Menu

Power Bar

Scroll Bars

Status Bar

Using the scroll bars

The document window is often not big enough to display all of its contents. To bring out-of-sight information into view, you use the scroll bars. Clicking the arrow at the end of a scroll bar moves the window's contents a small distance in the direction of the arrow. Clicking on either side of a scroll box (located in each scroll bar) moves the contents one windowful. The position of the scroll box in relation to the scroll bar indicates the position of the window in relation to its contents. Drag the scroll box to see specific parts of a document; for example, the middle or end.

If this is the very first time you've started WordPerfect, you'll be invited to run through a brief tutorial called the QuickStart Coach. Click No to skip the tutorial. (You can always run through the tutorial at a later time by choosing the Coaches command from the Help menu. See page 7 for more information about choosing commands.)

At the top of the window, the *title bar* tells you that you are looking at Document1 and that you have not yet modified the document. As soon as you type something or choose a command, *unmodified* will disappear, letting you know that the document has changed since you last saved it. Below the title bar is a *menu bar* from which you choose commands. Next comes the *Toolbar* and the *Power Bar*, which give you point-and-click access to WordPerfect's most frequently used commands. Across the bottom of the window is the *status bar*, which is divided into areas called *fields*. In the left field, *Insert* means that any characters you type will be inserted in the document. Next to *Insert* WordPerfect displays the currently selected printer followed by the date and time. In the right field, *Pg* tells you which page you are on (in this case, page 1); and *Ln* and *Pos* state your position, in inches, from the top and left margins of the page.

About an inch from the upper-left corner of the blank window sits the *insertion point* (the blinking vertical bar). The insertion point shows you where the action is—where the next character you type will be inserted or which character will be deleted if you press the Delete key. You also see your *mouse pointer*, which is an I-beam when it is over the blank window and a white arrow when it is anywhere else on the screen. The mouse pointer shows the location of the mouse relative to the screen and moves independently of the insertion point.

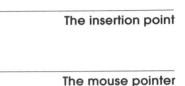

The insertion point

The mouse pointer

Now let's get down to business. So that you will have a document to work with, type the following note, but don't press Enter to start a new line. In case you're new to computers, you use the Shift key to enter capital (uppercase) letters and the Backspace key to erase mistakes. As you type, note the changes in the status bar.

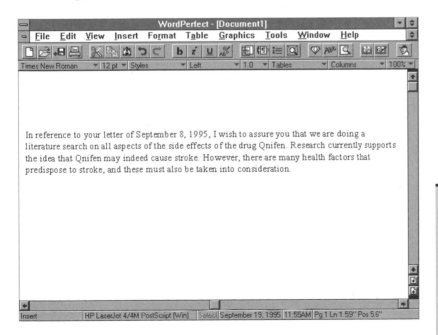

Starting over

If you make a mistake while creating the note (or any other document in this book) and want to start over in a clear window, simply choose the Close command from the File menu, and then click No when WordPerfect asks whether you want to save the document. (See page 7 if you need help choosing commands.)

As each line of text reaches the right edge of the screen, the next word you type moves to a new line. This is called *word wrapping*.

Moving Around the Screen

Navigating with
the mouse

You can move around the screen in a variety of ways. The easiest way is to use your mouse to quickly move the insertion point anywhere in a document. Simply position the I-beam pointer at the desired location, and click the left mouse button. The mouse really shines when you want to move around a document that is longer than the screen. To move to a location that is currently out of view, use the mouse and the scroll bar (see the tip on page 2) on the right side of the window to display the desired part of the document on the screen, and then click the mouse button to position the insertion point.

Navigating with
the keyboard

You can also use the keyboard to move around. Pressing the Up, Down, Left, and Right Arrow keys moves the insertion point up and down one line and left and right one character. But moving a line or character at a time is not the most efficient way to get around. Here are some faster ways:

To move the insertion point...	Press...
Left one word	Ctrl+Left Arrow
Right one word	Ctrl+Right Arrow
To beginning of line	Home
To beginning of line before codes	Home, Home
To end of line	End
Up one paragraph	Ctrl+Up Arrow
Down one paragraph	Ctrl+Down Arrow
To top of screen (then up a screen)	PgUp
To bottom of screen (then down a screen)	PgDn
Up one page	Alt+PgUp
Down one page	Alt+PgDn
To beginning of document	Ctrl+Home
To beginning of document before codes	Ctrl+Home, Ctrl+Home
To end of document	Ctrl+End

Try using various keys and key combinations to move around the note, rejoining us when you're reasonably "mobile."

Selecting Text

Knowing how to select text efficiently saves you time because you can then edit and apply formatting to blocks of text, instead of having to deal with individual characters. Follow along as we demonstrate selecting text blocks of different shapes and sizes, first with the mouse:

Keyboard conventions

When two keys are separated by a plus sign, such as Ctrl+Right Arrow, press and hold down the first key, and then press the second key. When two or more keys are separated by commas, such as Ctrl+Home,Ctrl+Home, press and release each key or key combination in the order in which it appears in the instruction.

1. Point to the first word of the note, and double-click the mouse button to select the word.

2. Point to the word *currently* in the second sentence, and triple-click the mouse button to select the sentence containing that word.

3. Point to any word, and quadruple-click (click four times) to select the entire paragraph.

4. Move the mouse pointer to the left of the first line of your document, and when the pointer changes to a white arrow, click to select the first sentence, and then double-click to select the paragraph.

   You don't have to select discreet units like words, sentences, or paragraphs. If you are skilled with your mouse, you can drag through the text itself to highlight exactly as much or as little as you need. You can also use your mouse in conjunction with the Shift key, like this:

1. Click an insertion point just before the word *we* in the first sentence.

Shift-clicking to select text

2. Point to the left of the period at the end of the sentence, hold down the Shift key, and click the mouse button. WordPerfect highlights all the characters between the two clicks:

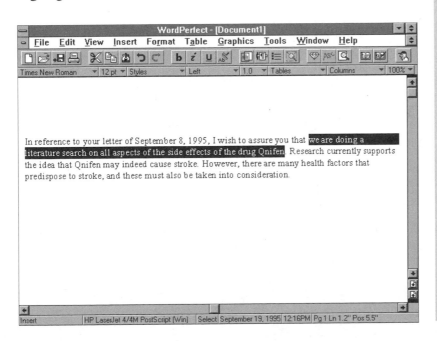

Selecting text with commands

Sometimes you might find it easier to select a specific unit of text by using a command. Choosing Select from the Edit menu displays a submenu from which you can choose Sentence, Paragraph, Page, or All. (The Select All command is particularly useful for selecting all the text in a long document.) If your text includes lists of items that you have created using tabs or indents, you can select a "column" of text by choosing Select and then Tabular Column. You can also select a block of text by choosing Select and then Rectangle.

3. Click anywhere in the note to remove the highlight.

Now let's look at a couple of keyboard selection methods:

Select mode

1. Press the F8 key to turn on Select mode. In the status bar, WordPerfect tells you that the mode is active.

2. Press the Right, Left, Up, and Down Arrow keys to select blocks of text of various shapes and sizes.

3. Try using several of the navigation key combinations listed in the table on page 4 in conjunction with Select mode to see their effects.

4. Press F8 again to turn off Select mode.

Selecting with Shift key combinations

When Select mode is not turned on, you can use the Shift key with other keys to highlight specific units of text. Here's a list of some of these units and the keys that select them:

To select...	Press...
A character left	Shift+Left Arrow
A character right	Shift+Right Arrow
A word left	Shift+Ctrl+Left Arrow
A word right	Shift+Ctrl+Right Arrow
A line up	Shift+Up Arrow
A line down	Shift+Down Arrow
A paragraph up	Shift+Ctrl+Up Arrow
A paragraph down	Shift+Ctrl+Down Arrow
A screen up	Shift+PgUp
A screen down	Shift+PgDn
A page up	Shift+Alt+PgUp
A page down	Shift+Alt+PgDn
To beginning of line	Shift+Home
To end of line	Shift+End
To beginning of document	Shift+Ctrl+Home
To end of document	Shift+Ctrl+End

Giving Instructions

You can give WordPerfect instructions in three ways: using menu commands, using shortcut keys and key combinations, and using buttons on the Toolbar and Power Bar. We'll look briefly at all three methods in this section.

Using Menu Commands

With earlier DOS versions of WordPerfect, you gave most instructions by using various keys and key combinations. Now the emphasis has shifted away from the keyboard and toward the mouse. Instead of having to remember the key combination for carrying out an action, you can give instructions visually, by choosing commands from menus. Try this:

1. Move the mouse pointer over the word *View* on the menu bar and click the left mouse button once to display the View menu. Some of the commands on this menu are preceded by check marks, indicating that the commands are toggles that can be turned on and off (a checked command is turned on). Others are followed by key combinations, indicating that pressing that combination activates the command without displaying the menu. You can close a menu without choosing a command by clicking outside the menu or pressing Esc or Alt.

   Displaying menus

   Closing menus

2. Move the mouse pointer over the Rulcr Bar command on the View menu, and click the left mouse button to display WordPerfect's ruler, which you use to set such layout elements as margins, indents, and tabs (see page 109 for more information about the Ruler Bar):

   Choosing commands

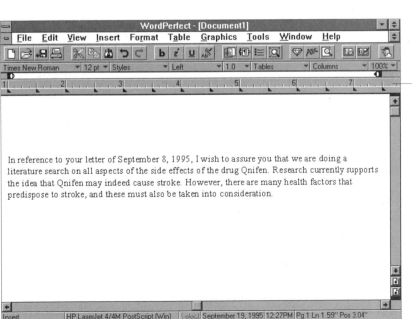

Ruler Bar

Choosing commands with the keyboard

From the keyboard, you can press Alt to activate the menu bar and then press the underlined letter of the name of the menu you want to open. To move among menus, use the Left and Right Arrow keys. When you have located the command you want to use, press its underlined letter to choose it.

Submenus

3. Click the word *Edit* on the menu bar. As you can see, some of the Edit-menu commands are followed by arrowheads. When you choose a command followed by an arrowhead, a *submenu* listing more commands appears. You choose a command from a submenu the same way you choose one from a regular menu. Other commands are followed by an ellipsis (...). An ellipsis indicates that when you choose the command, a *dialog box* will appear so that you can give WordPerfect the additional information it needs to carry out the command.

Dialog boxes

4. Choose the Preferences command from the Edit menu to display the Preferences dialog box:

5. To tell WordPerfect what type of preferences you want to work with, you double-click an icon-in this case, the Environment icon. WordPerfect displays this Environment Preferences dialog box:

Edit boxes

In this dialog box, you can type information in an *edit box*; for example, you can enter your name in the Name edit box.

You turn some options on or off by clicking the adjacent *check box* (an X means the option is turned on); for example, you can tell WordPerfect to beep your computer when an error occurs by clicking the Error check box in the Beep On group box. You select from a *pop-up list* of options by pointing to the arrows to the right of the option, holding down the mouse button, moving the highlight to the desired item, and then releasing the mouse button; for example, you can use this technique to change the Hyphenation Prompt option. You select from a set of *mutually exclusive options* by clicking one round button in a set; for example, you can select only one of the options in the Save Workspace group box at a time. In the upper-right corner of the dialog box are four *command buttons*. Clicking a command button that is followed by an ellipsis displays yet another dialog box with more choices.

Check boxes

Pop-up lists

Mutually exclusive options

Command buttons

6. Click the Code Page button to display this dialog box:

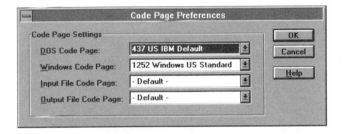

For advanced users: Custom menu bars

You can create custom menu bars and menus so that features you use frequently are easily accessible. Right-click the menu bar, and choose Preferences from the QuickMenu. Then click the Create button, and in the Create Menu Bar dialog box, type a name for the new menu bar, and click OK to display the Menu Bar Editor. Now you can edit the menu bar. Remove a menu you don't need by simply dragging it off the menu bar and releasing the mouse button when you see the trash can icon. Add a menu by dragging the Menu icon in the bottom-right corner of the dialog box to where you want it on the menu bar; double-click the new menu to edit its name. To add features to the new menu, start with the Activate A Feature option selected at the top of the Menu Bar Editor dialog box. (You can select Play A Keyboard Script, Launch A Program, or Play A Macro to add other types of actions to the menu.) Then select a menu name from the Feature Categories drop-down list, select an item from the Features list, and drag the item to the new menu. When the menu drops down, move the pointer to the location where you want to insert the selected item, and release the mouse button to add the item to the menu. To move an item from one menu to another, pull down the menu where the item is currently located, and drag the item to the desired location on the new menu. When the menu is complete, click OK, and then click Select to return to your document with the custom menu bar displayed. After you have created a menu bar, you can edit it by selecting it in the Menu Bar Preferences dialog box and clicking Edit to display the Menu Bar Editor; you can't edit the built-in WordPerfect menu bar.

You use the Code Page Preferences options to select a character set for documents in languages other than English. You change each option by clicking the arrow at the right end of its edit box to display a *drop-down list* of possible settings. If the list is longer than the list box, you use the scroll bar to the right of the box to bring more settings into view.

Drop-down lists

7. Click Cancel to close the Code Page Preferences dialog box without changing its settings, and then click Cancel to close the Environment Preferences dialog box. (To implement any changes you make in a dialog box, click OK or press Enter.)

8. Click Close to close the Preferences dialog box.

You'll practice using all these methods of giving information as we work our way through the book.

Using QuickMenus

QuickMenus group together the commands you are likely to use for an element of a document or window. You access a QuickMenu by pointing to the element and clicking the right mouse button. To see how QuickMenus work, try this:

Right-clicking to display QuickMenus

1. Point to the Ruler Bar, and click the right mouse button once. (From now on, we'll refer to this action as *right-clicking*.) WordPerfect displays the Ruler Bar's QuickMenu, listing all the actions you are most likely to perform with the Ruler Bar.

2. Choose Hide Ruler Bar from the QuickMenu. WordPerfect removes the Ruler Bar from the screen.

Throughout this book, we'll use QuickMenus whenever they are the most efficient way of accomplishing a particular task.

Using Shortcut Key Combinations

With WordPerfect for Windows, you can use Ctrl, Shift, and Alt key combinations to give instructions. Try the following:

1. Hold down Alt+Shift, and press F3 to redisplay the Ruler Bar.

2. Click View in the menu bar. The Ruler Bar toggle command is now preceded by a check mark. Choose the command to turn off the Ruler Bar.

Using the Toolbar and Power Bar

The Toolbar and Power Bar provide point-and-click ways of carrying out common word-processing tasks with the mouse.

The Toolbar

The buttons on the Toolbar provide instant access to Word-Perfect features that enable you to create professional-looking documents. To give an instruction using the Toolbar, you click the appropriate button. If WordPerfect needs more information before it can carry out the instruction, it displays a dialog box, just as if you had chosen the corresponding command from a menu. First let's see what each button does:

1. Move the mouse pointer to the leftmost button on the Toolbar. WordPerfect displays the button's name—in this case, New Blank Document—in a box below the pointer and a brief description of the button's action in the title bar. This helpful feature is called *QuickTips*.

QuickTips

2. Move the pointer to each button in turn to display its name.

   Now let's see how to use one of the buttons:

1. Press Ctrl+Home to move to the beginning of the note.

2. Click the Page/Zoom Full button on the Toolbar. WordPerfect displays the note as a full page on the screen, like this:

The Page/Zoom Full button

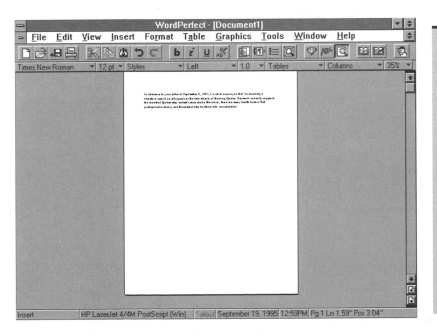

Feature Bars

In addition to placing commonly used commands within easy reach on the Toolbars and Power Bar, WordPerfect uses Feature Bars to provide easy access to the commands you'll use with specific features, such as tables, footnotes, and outlines. When you activate these features, WordPerfect automatically displays the corresponding Feature Bar below the Power Bar. We'll work with several different feature bars in the course of this book.

3. Click the Page/Zoom Full button again to return to normal Page view.

If a Toolbar contains more buttons than can fit on the screen at one time, you can scroll the out-of-sight buttons into view by clicking the arrows at the right end of the Toolbar.

WordPerfect comes with 13 Toolbars, each with a combination of buttons that is most appropriate for a particular kind of task. For example, the Graphics Toolbar contains the buttons you are most likely to need when creating and manipulating graphics. You can also create your own Toolbar by assigning commands to buttons, arranging the buttons on a bar to suit your fancy, and then saving the custom Toolbar for future use. You can display the Toolbar across the top of your screen—the default position—or you can specify that it appear elsewhere. And your buttons can sport names, pictures, or both. Let's experiment:

Changing the Toolbar look and location

1. Point to the Toolbar, right-click the mouse, choose Preferences from the group of commands at the bottom of the menu, and then click the Options button to display this dialog box:

Changing the Toolbar position and shape

The Toolbar is not limited to the locations specified in the Toolbar Options dialog box. You can drag the Toolbar anywhere in the document window by pointing to the vertical border between two buttons or to a blank area of the bar, holding down the left mouse button, and dragging to the desired location. When you drag anywhere other than to the top, bottom, left, or right edge of the window, the Toolbar changes from a bar to a rectangular palette.

2. Select Text in the Appearance group box and Left in the Location group box, click OK to close the Toolbar Options dialog box, and then click Close to close the Toolbar Preferences dialog box. Here's the result:

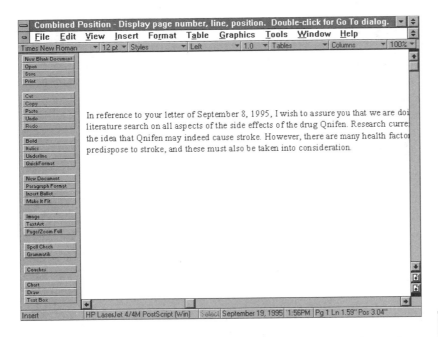

3. Right-click the Toolbar, choose Preferences again, select Options, reset the Appearance setting to Picture and the Location setting to Top, and click OK, leaving the Toolbar Preferences dialog box open.

Now let's add a button to the active Toolbar:

1. In the Available Toolbars list, *6.1 WordPerfect* is highlighted because the WordPerfect Toolbar is active. Without moving the highlight, click the Edit button to display this dialog box:

For advanced users: Custom Toolbars

To create a custom Toolbar, right-click the Toolbar, and choose Preferences from the Quick-Menu. Then click the Create button, and in the Create Toolbar dialog box, type a name for the new Toolbar, and click OK to display the Toolbar Editor. Now you can assemble your Toolbar. With the Activate A Feature option selected at the top of the dialog box, select a menu from the Feature Categories drop-down list, select an item from the Features list, and either click Add Button or drag the item to the Toolbar. You can select Play A Keyboard Script, Launch A Program, or Play A Macro to add other types of actions to the Toolbar. When the Toolbar is complete, click OK, and then click Select to return to your document with the custom Toolbar displayed on your screen.

(You can also access this dialog box by right-clicking the Toolbar and choosing Edit from the QuickMenu.) Word-Perfect assumes you want to add a feature button, and by default, lists all the features you can access through the File menu. You can select other menus from the Feature Categories drop-down list to display their features.

2. Scroll the Features list box until Document Info comes into view. (The Document Info command on the File menu gives you information about the current document such as the number of characters and lines and the maximum number of words per sentence.)

3. Point to Document Info and hold down the left mouse button. When the button-and-hand icon appears, drag the icon up to the left end of the Toolbar, and release the mouse button. WordPerfect adds a Document Information button to the Toolbar.

Moving buttons →

4. With the Toolbar Editor still on your screen, locate the New Document and Paragraph Format buttons on the Toolbar.

5. Now point to the Document Information button, hold down the mouse button, drag the Document Information button to the right so that it sits over both the New Document and the Paragraph Format buttons, and release the mouse button. WordPerfect rearranges the Toolbar, placing the Document Information button between the New Document and Paragraph Format buttons.

6. Click OK to close the Toolbar Editor dialog box, and then click Close to close the Toolbar Preferences dialog box. The Toolbar now looks like this:

> ### Deleting buttons and Toolbars
>
> To delete a button from a Toolbar, right-click the Toolbar, and then choose Edit from the Quick-Menu. Next, point to the button you want to delete, hold down the left mouse button, and drag the button away from the Toolbar. Release the mouse button when you see the small trash can icon. To delete a Toolbar, right-click the Toolbar, and choose Preferences from the Quick-Menu. Highlight the Toolbar you want to delete, click the Delete button, and then click Yes to confirm the deletion.

Document Information button

7. Next click the Document Information button to display this dialog box: Displaying document statistics

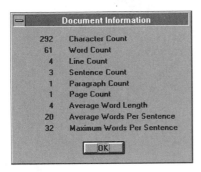

8. Click OK when you have finished perusing the document information.

The Power Bar

You can use the Power Bar to quickly carry out a number of common formatting tasks. You could perform these tasks by choosing commands from menus, but clicking buttons and selecting options from the pop-up lists on the Power Bar is usually more efficient. We'll put several Power Bar buttons through their paces in the next chapter.

After you gain more experience with WordPerfect for Windows, you may find that you rarely use some of the buttons or that you often use commands not currently represented by buttons on the Power Bar. You can change the buttons using techniques similar to those described for the Toolbar. However, you can't change the position of the Power Bar. Customizing the Power Bar

Saving Documents

You probably know that the note you have typed and edited currently exists in your computer's memory and that this memory (called *RAM* for *random access memory*) is temporary. All information in RAM is wiped out when you turn off your computer. To move the note to a more permanent storage place, you have to save it.

When you save a document for the first time, WordPerfect asks you to supply a filename. Using up to eight characters, you should try to come up with a name that reflects the

Filename characters

Here's a list of the characters you can use in filenames:

A-Z
0-9
! @ # $ % & ( ) - ' ' _

WordPerfect might accept other characters in filenames or extensions, but sticking with these characters ensures that all your filenames will be valid.

contents of the document you're saving. And you should be consistent. For example, you might want to assign similar names to documents connected with the same project so that they are readily identifiable as part of that project. To further identify the contents of a file, WordPerfect adds the extension WPD to every file created in WordPerfect. You can add your own extension, but it must be preceded by a period and have no more than three characters. For example, you can use the extensions LET (for letters) and MEM (for memos). Do not use BAT, COM, and EXE, which are reserved for program files.

Enough philosophizing. Let's save the note:

1. With the note displayed on your screen, choose the Save As command from the File menu to display this dialog box:

2. In the Filename edit box, type the filename (use *note* for this example), and press Enter. WordPerfect saves the file and displays its abbreviated pathname in the title bar at the top of the document window. Notice that WordPerfect has automatically appended the WPD extension to the filename.

The Save button

After you've saved the document and given it a name, you can click the Save button on the Toolbar or use the Save command on the File menu to save subsequent changes. Choose Save As only if you want to assign a different name to a new version of the document. Don't ever hesitate to use Save. It may *save* your bacon some day.

Backing Up Files

To spare you the trauma of losing work because of machine failures or power outages, or because you somehow managed to make a mess of a document, you should regularly back up, or make copies of, your files. While you are creating a document, you can back it up by turning on the Original Document Backup option and then saving the file regularly, or you can have WordPerfect automatically back up your files using its Timed Document Backup option. We discuss both methods in this section.

Retaining the Previous Version of a Document

Each time you save a file, the current version overwrites the previous version. By turning on the Original Document Backup option, you can tell WordPerfect to change the extension of the previous version of the file to BK! so that you can save both the current and previous versions. By default, WordPerfect stores the backup file in the same directory as the current version.

Here's how to activate the Original Document Backup option:

1. Choose the Preferences command from the Edit menu.

2. Double-click the File icon to display this dialog box:

Pathnames

A file's pathname includes its filename as well as its "address." For example, C:\OFFICE\WPWIN\WPDOCS\NOTE.WPD tells us that the NOTE.WPD file is located in the WPDOCS subdirectory of the WPWIN directory, which branches from the main, (root), directory of drive C. By default, WordPerfect saves your documents in the WPDOCS subdirectory. To specify another directory, choose Preferences from the Edit menu, double-click the File icon, and specify a new location in the Default Directory edit box in the File Preferences dialog box.

By default, the Documents/Backup option is selected in the top part of the File Preferences dialog box, and its settings are displayed in the lower part. Selecting another option in the top part of the dialog box changes the settings in the lower part to those that are available for the selected option.

3. Click the Original Document Backup check box, and then click OK.

4. Click Close in the Preferences dialog box to return to the document window.

5. Now save NOTE.WPD by clicking the Save button on the Toolbar. WordPerfect saves the original version of the file as NOTE.BK! and the current version as NOTE.WPD.

The next time you save NOTE.WPD, WordPerfect will delete NOTE.BK!, save NOTE.WPD as NOTE.BK!, and save the new version of the note as NOTE.WPD. Then if NOTE.WPD is accidentally damaged or deleted, you can always retrieve NOTE.BK!, rename it NOTE.WPD, and quickly reconstruct any changes you have made since the last time you saved the document.

Making Timed Backups

By default, WordPerfect's Timed Document Backup option automatically saves your work every 10 minutes. If you are working with more than one document, WordPerfect creates a backup file for each of them (WP{WP}.BK1 for document 1, WP{WP}.BK2 for document 2, and so on). Backup files are stored in the main WordPerfect directory unless you specify another directory. If you lose the current version of your work, through a power outage for example, you can retrieve the backup file and pick up where you left off. WordPerfect deletes these backup files when you end your current work session.

If you decide that 10 minutes is too long an interval between backups, you can change the interval as follows:

Timed backup directory

To store your timed backup files in a different directory, type the name of the desired directory in the Backup Directory edit box of the File Preferences dialog box. For example, to store backup files in a special BACKUP directory, type *c:\office\wpwin\backup.* (The BACKUP directory must already exist on your hard drive.)

1. Choose Preferences from the Edit menu, and double-click the File icon to display the File Preferences dialog box.

Changing the timed backup interval

2. In the Timed Document Backup Every edit box, type the desired time interval, and click OK. In the Preferences dialog box, click Close to return to your document.

Opening Documents

To give you some practice in opening existing WordPerfect for Windows documents, let's open the NOTE.BK! file that WordPerfect created when you last saved the note. Follow these steps:

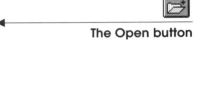

The Open button

1. Click the Open button on the Toolbar to display a dialog box like this one:

The files listed are stored in the directory specified above the QuickList box. If the file you want is not stored in the current directory, you need to switch to the correct directory in order to select the file. You would double-click C:\ to display the root directory's files and subdirectories; double-click a sub-directory to display its files and subdirectories; and so on.

2. For this example, simply double-click NOTE.BK! in the list of filenames. WordPerfect opens the previous version of the note in its own window.

File open shortcut

If the file you want to open is one of the four most recently opened files, you can bypass the Open File dialog box and simply choose the file from the bottom of the File menu.

Creating New Documents

You now have two documents open on your screen, though NOTE.WPD is totally obscured by NOTE.BK!. For good measure, let's open a third document, this time a brand new one. There's just one step:

The New Blank Document button

1. Click the New Blank Document button on the Toolbar.

That's all there is to it! A new blank document is displayed in a window, on top of NOTE.BK! and NOTE.WPD. This document is based on WordPerfect's standard template, which specifies the default font, size, and the margins. (See page 28 for more information about templates.)

Manipulating Windows

Now that we have a few windows to play with, we'll pause here to review some window basics. Being able to work with more than one document open at a time is useful, especially if you need to use the same information in different documents. For example, you might use the same text in a memo, a letter, and a legal brief. Follow these steps to see how easy it is to move from one document to another:

Navigating between windows

If your hands are on the keyboard, you can move quickly from one window to another by pressing Ctrl+F6 to move to the window of the next document or pressing Ctrl+Shift+F6 to move to the window of the previous document. (*Next* and *previous* are determined by the order in which the documents were opened.)

1. Click *Window* on the menu bar to display the Window menu, which lists the three open documents.

2. Choose NOTE.WPD from the list of open documents. WordPerfect brings the current version of the note to the top of the stack of windows.

3. Next choose Tile Horizontal from the Window menu. WordPerfect arranges the three open documents so that they each occupy about a third of the screen, as shown here:

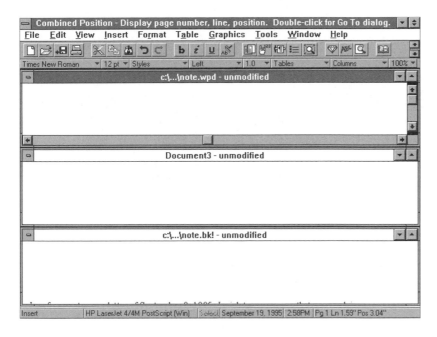

4. Click anywhere in the NOTE.BK! window to activate it.
   Notice that the title bar of the active document is a different
   color from the other two title bars and that scroll bars appear
   only in the active window. Any entries you make and any
   commands you choose will affect only the active document.

5. Click the Maximize button (the upward-pointing arrowhead)
   in the upper-right corner of the NOTE.BK! window. The
   window expands to fill the screen, completely obscuring the
   other two documents.

   Maximizing a window

6. Click the Open button on the Toolbar, and double-click
   NOTE.BK! to open a second copy of the file. (Opening two
   copies of the same document lets you view different parts at
   the same time.) WordPerfect tells you that the second copy
   will be read-only and that you will not be able to modify it
   without changing its name. Click Yes to open the copy.

   Opening a second copy of a document

7. Verify that you have two copies of the same document open
   by clicking *Window* on the menu bar. At the bottom of the
   menu, a second version of NOTE.BK! is listed.

Cascading windows ────────►
8. Choose Cascade from the open Window menu. WordPerfect arranges the document windows like this:

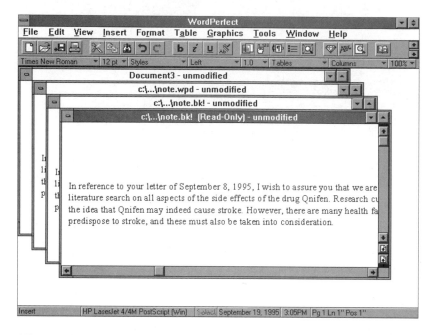

These simple techniques work equally well no matter how many documents you have open. (You can have nine documents open at one time, but three or four is the practical limit.)

Closing Documents

When you've finished working with a document, it's wise to close it to conserve your computer's memory. In this section, we'll show you three ways to close documents:

1. With the second copy of NOTE.BK! still active, click the small dash in the box at the left end of its title bar to display the Document Control menu, and then choose Close. WordPerfect closes the document.

2. With NOTE.BK! active, choose the Close command from the File menu. (If you have made changes to this document, WordPerfect asks whether to save the document. Click No.)

3. Finally, choose Document3 from the Window menu, and then press Ctrl+F4, the Close command's shortcut key combination. (Again, click No if you're asked about saving changes.)

The current version of the memo (NOTE.WPD) is now the only document open on your screen.

Getting Help

With WordPerfect for Windows, help is never far away. If you get stuck, you have several options, depending on what level of information you need. At the "memory jogger" end of the spectrum are the document window's title bar, which offers brief explanations of the highlighted command or the button to which you are pointing, and the status bar, which gives on-the-spot information about the status of some features. At the other end of the spectrum is the comprehensive reference manual. In between is WordPerfect's Help feature, which we'll briefly look at here.

The Help Feature

You can access the WordPerfect for Windows Help feature by choosing commands from the Help menu at the right end of the menu bar. The type of information displayed depends on which command you choose and what you are doing in WordPerfect at the time. The best way to explore the Help feature is to have WordPerfect itself show you around. Here's how to ask for a guided tour:

1. Choose the Contents command from the Help menu to display the Help window, and then click the window's Maximize button so that the window fills the entire screen, as shown on the next page.

Getting help with Help

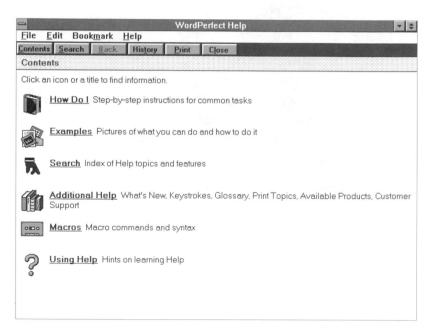

2. Click Using Help at the bottom of the window to display information about the Help feature, as shown here:

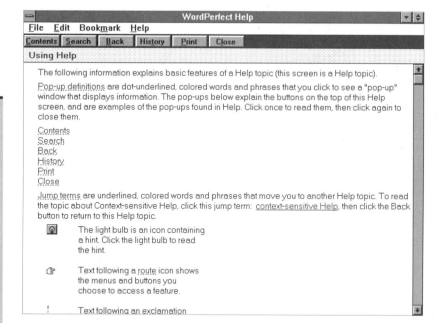

Coaches

To get step-by-step instructions on how to perform certain tasks in WordPerfect, you can enlist the help of a coach or two. Just choose Coaches from the Help menu, and when the Coaches dialog box appears, select a lesson from the list of those available, and click OK. The coach then guides you through the steps involved in performing the task. (And this coach won't make you sit on the sidelines if you make a mistake.)

3. Read the information in the window, and then click the words with dotted underlines to display pop-up windows with information about the buttons on the Help window's Toolbar.

4. Click the Back button on the Help window's Toolbar to return to the Contents window, and take a moment to investigate other Help topics.

5. When you are ready, click the Close button to return to the document window.

Context-Sensitive Help

WordPerfect can give you *context-sensitive help* by displaying a Help window containing information about a particular command or dialog box. For example, suppose you want information about the Preferences command. You simply click the Edit menu, use the Down Arrow key to move the highlight to the Preferences command, and then press the F1 key to display a Help window with information about the command. If you have already chosen the Preferences command and want to find out more before you proceed, you can click the Help button in the Preferences dialog box to display the same information. (All dialog boxes have a Help button, so help with an option is never more than a mouse click away.)

Quitting WordPerfect for Windows

Well, that's it for the basic tour. We'll finish up by showing you how to end a WordPerfect for Windows session:

1. Choose Exit from the File menu.

2. If WordPerfect asks whether you want to save the changes you have made to the open document, click Yes.

Upgrade Expert

On WordPerfect's Help menu, you'll find the Upgrade Expert command. When you choose this command, the Upgrade Expert dialog box walks you through the steps necessary to make a smooth transition from your old word processor to WordPerfect 6.1 for Windows. (You can also request to see a list of WordPerfect's newest features.)

2

Quick and Easy Documents: Writing a Memo

Use WordPerfect's templates to quickly create professional-looking documents

MEMO

To: Dr. George Winters
From: Dr. Kaye Fox
Subject: Case #312
Date: September 18, 1995

The woman who is the complainant in Case #312 was seen by Dr. Reynolds on August 9. At that time he noted that she had been a smoker for over 30 years. This is a new development, which I think we should investigate thoroughly.

Attached is an article from the New World Journal of Medicine on the association of cigarette smoking and the incidence of stroke in patients using the drug Qnifen. This is an up-to-date study from the University of Reedsport School of Medicine. Research currently supports the idea that Qnifen may indeed cause stroke. However, there are many health factors that predispose to stroke, and these must also be taken into consideration. Please review the article and give me your reaction as soon as possible.

Correct your text with simple editing techniques

Incorporate text from other documents

Copy or move words, sentences, or paragraphs with a few mouse clicks

With the advent of word processors, memos are easier to create than ever before. No more scribbled or laboriously typed notes. You can now turn out—in no time at all—neat, error-free memos recording who said what to whom, calling a meeting, or announcing a new policy. In the next few pages, we show you how to write, edit, and print a memo based on one of WordPerfect for Windows' memo templates. This template provides a basic memo structure (title, headings, and message area) that you can use again and again, plugging in new information each time.

WordPerfect provides several template files as starting points for the documents you create. In addition to the memo templates, you'll find templates for letters, faxes, newsletters, and other standard documents. The template files all have descriptive names, so it's easy to locate the type of template you're looking for. In Chapter 4, we'll show you how to create a template and add it to WordPerfect's template "library."

The memo template we'll use is a plain, businesslike memo, but there is no reason why you shouldn't add a personal touch or two. After reading the other chapters in this book, you'll be able to dress up the memo template with borders or graphics, but for now, we'll keep things simple. Just remember that with WordPerfect, you can customize templates to meet your needs.

Using WordPerfect's Templates

Before you open the memo template, be sure your screen is clear. If you're at the DOS prompt, type *win* to load Windows, double-click the WPWin 6.1 icon, and then double-click the WordPerfect icon to start WordPerfect for Windows. If a document is displayed on your screen, choose Close from the File menu. (If you've made any changes since the last time you saved the document, WordPerfect asks whether you want to save those changes; click Yes or No as appropriate.) That's it. Now for the memo:

The New Document button

1. Click the New Document button on the Toolbar or choose the New command from the File menu to display this dialog box:

2. Select Memo in the Group list box and then select Menu -
Traditional in the Select Template list.

3. Click the Select button. If this is the first time you have opened
a template, you see a message box asking whether you want
to personalize the template. Click OK, and then enter the
following information in the appropriate edit boxes, pressing
Enter to move from one box to another and to skip the boxes
you want to leave blank:

 ← **Entering personal information**

Name:	*Dr. Kaye Fox*
Organization:	*Fox & Associates*
Address:	*1224 Evergreen Road*
City, State, Zip:	*Lake Oswego, OR 97035*
Telephone:	*(503) 555-4567*

After you've completed the exercises in this book, you can
go back and enter your own personal information by clicking
the Personal Info button that appears in some template dialog
boxes. As you'll soon see, WordPerfect uses this information
in any templates that require it, such as memos and letters.

4. Click the OK button. WordPerfect displays this Template
Information dialog box:

WordPerfect experts

Some of WordPerfect's templates
come with "roadside" assistance
in the form of "experts." Using a
series of dialog boxes, these experts walk you through the process of creating documents like
memos and letters. The experts
also provide assistance with more
complicated tasks, such as faxing
and adding watermarks (see the
tip on page 74). When you select
a template group in the New
Document dialog box, an expert
(if available) appears at the top
of the Select Template list. Just
double-click the expert's name,
and follow the directions in the
corresponding dialog box(es).
For more information about
WordPerfect experts, see Chapter
4, where we use the Letter Expert.

Filling in the memo's headings

5. In the Name Of Recipient(s) edit box, type *Dr. George Winters*, and click the Next Field button or press Enter.

6. In the Subject edit box, type *Case #312*, and then click OK. WordPerfect displays this document:

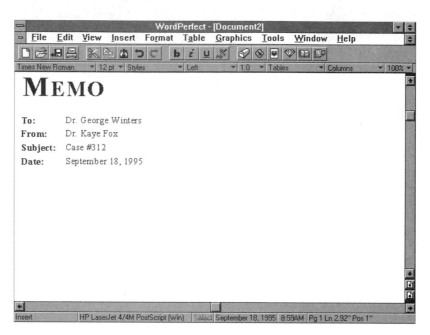

The correct date, every time

When you load WordPerfect's traditional memo template, the Date line is already filled in with the correct date. Why? Because this line of the template contains a Date code. When WordPerfect encounters a Date code, it replaces the code with the current date recorded by your computer's clock/calendar. You can insert Date codes in a document by positioning the insertion point where you want the date to appear and choosing Date and then Date Code from the Insert menu. If you want to change the format of any date you insert via a Date Code, position the mouse pointer before the date, choose Date and then Date Format from the Insert menu, and then select a new format in the Document Date/Time Format dialog box.

As you can see, a different Toolbar now spans your screen. WordPerfect has provided a Toolbar containing the features it thinks you are likely to use when writing a memo. Let's do that now:

1. The first thing to do is assign the memo a name. Click the Save button on the Toolbar. Because you have not yet given this file a name, WordPerfect displays the Save As dialog box, just as if you had chosen Save As from the File menu (see page 16).

2. Type *memo* and press Enter. (Remember, WordPerfect appends the WPD extension for you.)

3. Now type the memo's message. Press Ctrl+End and, using the graphic on the facing page as a guide, type the first paragraph, press Enter twice to end the paragraph and create a blank line, type the second paragraph, and press Enter again:

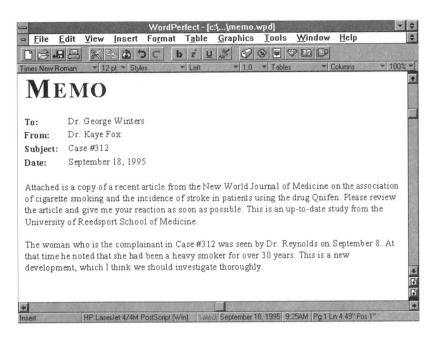

4. Click the Save button on the Toolbar to save your work.

Editing Basics

To complete the memo, you need to know some basic editing techniques. We'll start with the simplest methods and then move on to more advanced methods that will allow you to correct and revise your documents quickly and efficiently.

Deleting Text

You are probably already familiar with the Backspace key which deletes the character to the left of the insertion point. To delete the character to the right of the insertion point, you use the Delete key, which is located on the right side of your keyboard (some keyboards have a key labeled *Del*). You can delete more than one character at a time by selecting the text you want to delete and then pressing the Delete key.

If you accidentally delete the wrong item, don't panic. WordPerfect's Undo command was designed to avoid such catastrophies. Simply click the Undo button on the Toolbar or choose the Undo command from the Edit menu or press Ctrl+Z to undo your last action. (Bear in mind that some actions, such as saving a file, cannot be undone.)

Turning off the Toolbar

The sample memo is short enough to fit easily on the screen, but when you type longer documents, you might want to turn off the Toolbar so that you can see more of your text in the window at the same time. Simply right-click the Toolbar, and choose Hide Toolbar from the bottom of the Quick-Menu. To turn the Toolbar back on, you can choose Toolbar from the View menu.

Let's make some corrections to the text of the memo:

1. Double-click the word *recent* in the first sentence of the memo text and press Delete. Then type *n* to turn the *a* into *an*.

2. Click an insertion point after the word *heavy* in the second paragraph and press Ctrl+Backspace to delete the word.

3. Next, select the word *September* in the second paragraph and type *August*. The selected text is deleted automatically when you begin typing.

4. Triple-click the last sentence in the first paragraph of the memo to select the entire sentence and then press Delete. Oops. That's not what you meant to do!

The Undo button

5. To undelete the sentence, click the Undo button on the Toolbar. Whew!

Remember, Undo can be used to undo only your most recent action; you must click the Undo button or choose the Undo command from the Edit menu immediately after you've made a mistake. If you need to undo a previous action, you can use the Undo/Redo History command on the Edit menu (see the tip on the facing page).

Now suppose you decide that you really don't need the last sentence in the first paragraph of the memo. Try this:

The Redo button

1. Click the Redo button on the Toolbar to "redo" your undo.

2. Then click the Undo button again to restore the sentence once and for all.

Undeleting Text

In addition to the invaluable Undo, WordPerfect provides an Undelete command, which allows you to restore any or all of your previous three deletions at the insertion point. To see how Undelete works, first make these deletions:

1. Click an insertion point to the left of the *w* in *woman* in the second paragraph, hold down Shift, and click an insertion point to the left of the *c* in *complainant* to select the text

---

The QuickMenu for selected text

You can move, copy, and delete selected text by right-clicking the text and choosing the desired commands from the Quick-Menu. In addition, you can use the QuickMenu to apply common formatting to the selected text. (See Chapter 3 for more information about formatting.)

between the two clicks. Release the Shift key, and then press Delete.

2. Use the same technique to delete *a copy of* at the beginning of the first paragraph.

3. Now suppose you have second thoughts about deleting *woman who is the*. To undelete it, click an insertion point in front of the *c* in *complainant*, and choose Undelete from the Edit menu to display the Undelete dialog box:

Notice that WordPerfect has restored your most recent deletion (*a copy of*) at the insertion point.

4. Click the Previous button in the Undelete dialog box. The words *woman who is the* appear at the insertion point.

5. Click the Restore button to undelete this deletion.

Overtyping Errors

Another way to correct minor errors is to use WordPerfect's Typeover mode to overtype mistakes. Follow the steps on the next page to make a simple correction using Typeover.

The Undo/Redo History command

To undo or redo two or more editing actions at once, simply choose Undo/Redo History from the Edit menu, and select the action(s) you want to undo or redo in the Undo/Redo History dialog box. When you select an action, any actions listed above the selection are also highlighted and will be undone or redone when you click the Undo or Redo button. You control the number of items displayed in the Undo/Redo History dialog box by clicking the Options button in the dialog box, entering a number (from 0 to 300) in the Number Of Undo/Redo Items edit box, and clicking OK. You can save the Undo/Redo history with your document, but saving the history increases the size of the document file.

Typeover mode

1. Move the insertion point to the left of the *8* in *August 8*, and press the Insert (Ins) key to turn on Typeover mode. The word *Typeover* replaces *Insert* in the status bar at the bottom of your screen.

2. Type *9*. WordPerfect replaces the character to the right of the insertion point with the character you typed.

Insert mode

3. Press the Insert key again to turn off Typeover mode and turn on Insert mode.

4. Click the Save button to save your changes. From now on, we won't tell you when to save the memo; just remember to save frequently to safeguard your work.

Moving Text

When it comes to rearranging text, the Cut and Paste buttons on WordPerfect's Toolbar are really handy. They let you move blocks of text using just a few mouse clicks. Let's give it a try:

1. Click an insertion point anywhere in the last sentence of the first paragraph of the memo, and choose Select and then Sentence from the Edit menu. WordPerfect selects the entire sentence.

The Cut button

2. Click the Cut button on the Toolbar. WordPerfect deletes the highlighted sentence and moves it to a temporary storage place in your computer's memory called the *Clipboard*.

The Paste button

3. Click an insertion point to the left of the *P* in *Please review*, and click the Paste button on the Toolbar. The sentence reappears in its new location. (Notice that WordPerfect automatically inserts a space after the repositioned sentence.)

If you accidentally cut the wrong text, you can restore the text to its original location by choosing Undo *before* you reposition the insertion point and click Paste.

Using the Cut and Paste buttons to move text is easy enough, but WordPerfect offers an even faster way: Drag And Drop Text. This technique is convenient because only the mouse is involved—you don't have to bother with buttons, menus, or the keyboard. Using Drag And Drop Text, let's transpose the two paragraphs of the memo:

Moving with Drag And Drop Text

1. If necessary, use the scroll bar to adjust the screen so that you can see both of the memo's paragraphs. Click an insertion point in the second paragraph, and choose Select and then Paragraph from the Edit menu.

2. Position the mouse pointer anywhere in the selected paragraph. Then hold down the left mouse button, and drag the pointer—which now has a small gray box at its base—to just before the *A* in *Attached* at the beginning of the first paragraph. When you release the mouse button, this is the result:

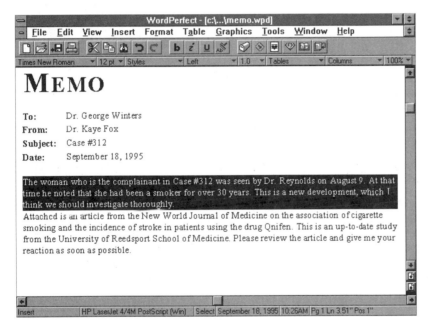

3. Click an insertion point before the *A* in *Attached*, and press Enter to insert a blank line between the two paragraphs.

You might think using Drag And Drop Text is a little awkward at first, but once you get the hang of it, you'll find it indispensable. So practice on your own, and before you know it, you'll be draggin' and droppin' every chance you get.

Copying Text

Next we'll use a similar technique to copy a block of text in the memo.

The Clipboard

The Windows Clipboard is a temporary storage space in your computer's memory. It is used to hold cut or copied information from all Windows applications. You can use it to transfer information from one place to another in a document, from one document to another, and from one application to another. The Clipboard can hold only one item of information at a time; cutting or copying a subsequent item overwrites the original Clipboard contents, so be sure to paste an item you need before performing another cut or copy operation. (Information erased with the Delete key is not stored on the Clipboard, so you can delete information using this key without disturbing the Clipboard's contents.) Because the Windows Clipboard is a temporary storage space, exiting Windows erases any information that is stored there.

The Copy button

1. With the insertion point still in the second paragraph of the memo, choose Select and then Paragraph from the Edit menu.

2. Click the Copy button on the Toolbar.

3. Press End, and if necessary press the Down Arrow key to move the insertion point to a blank line below the memo.

4. Click the Paste button. WordPerfect inserts a copy of the paragraph, as shown here:

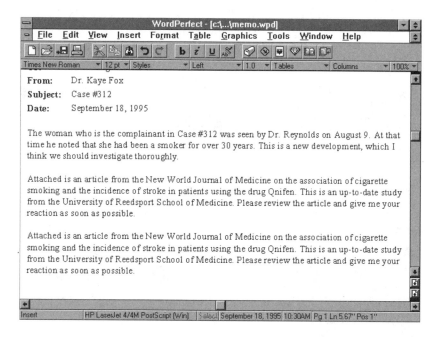

5. Now delete the second copy of the paragraph by selecting the paragraph and pressing Delete.

Copying with Drag And Drop Text

You can use Drag And Drop Text to copy text as well as move it. Simply select the text you want to copy, drag the copy to its new location, and hold down the Ctrl key before you release the mouse button.

Copying Text from Another Document

One of the real advantages of a word processor is that it enables you to use the same text in several different documents. You type the text once and then use the simple techniques just described to transfer copies of the text elsewhere. Let's copy part of the note you wrote in Chapter 1 and paste it into MEMO.WPD:

1. Click the Open button on the Toolbar or choose Open from the File menu.

2. In the Open File dialog box, click NOTE.WPD to highlight it, and then click the View button. WordPerfect opens a Viewer window in which it displays the contents of the selected file:

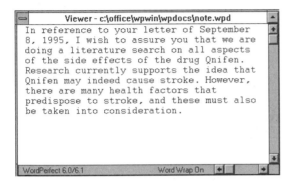

3. After verifying that this is the file you want, click OK. WordPerfect opens the note in its own document window.

4. In the note, click an insertion point to the left of the *R* in *Research*, and then press Shift+Ctrl+End to select the last two sentences of the note.

For advanced users: QuickFinder

The WordPerfect for Windows QuickFinder feature is designed to help you quickly locate documents based on their actual contents and/or their filenames or extensions. This powerful feature is particularly useful for businesses such as law firms or research organizations that sometimes need to extract related materials from huge numbers of files. To use QuickFinder, click the QuickFinder command button in a related dialog box such as the Open dialog box. You can then enter a word or phrase and then specify where WordPerfect is to conduct its search. Alternatively, you can give WordPerfect a filename or filename pattern to search for (for example, entering *.LET* tells WordPerfect to search for all files with the LET extension). Possible search limits include files in specific directories, files with dates falling in a particular range, and only files created in WordPerfect. The fastest way to search the actual contents of your documents is to use the QuickFinder Indexer to create indexes of all the significant words in the documents so that WordPerfect can search the indexes rather than the files themselves.

More about Viewer

Right-clicking the Viewer window displays a QuickMenu of Viewer options that allow you to do such things as see the format of the file you are viewing, search for words and phrases, change the font (in the Viewer window only), print the file, and wrap the file's text to fit the Viewer window.

5. Click the Copy button on the Toolbar to copy the two sentences, and choose Close from the File menu to close NOTE.WPD. (If WordPerfect asks whether you want to save changes to the note, click No.)

6. With the memo's window active, click an insertion point to the left of the *P* in *Please review* in the second paragraph, and then click the Paste button. The two sentences from the note are now incorporated in the memo, as shown here:

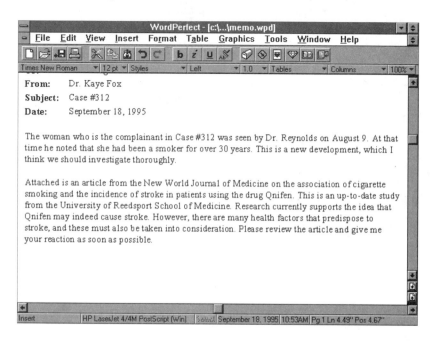

Printing Documents

When you installed WordPerfect for Windows, the installation program copied to your hard drive all the files necessary for WordPerfect and your printer to communicate. The printer we will use throughout this book is a Hewlett-Packard LaserJet 4M. If you are using a different printer, you might have a different choice of fonts. (We cover fonts in more detail on page 58.) Otherwise, you should have no difficulty printing the documents you create as you read this book.

Viewing the Memo

Before you actually print a document, you might want to see how it will look on the printed page. Page view shows your document as it will look when printed, but you can see only as much of the document as will fit on one screen at a time. To view your document a full page at a time, you use WordPerfect's Zoom feature. Try the following:

1. Press Ctrl+Home to move to the top of the memo, and then click the Zoom button on the Power Bar to display a drop-down list of magnification options.

The Zoom button

2. Select Full Page from the drop-down list. Here is the result:

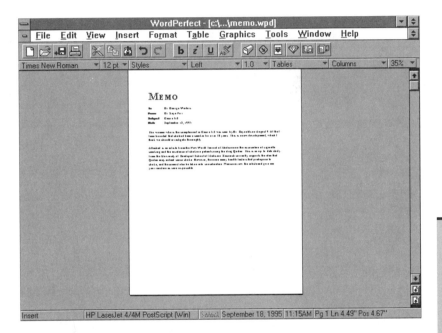

3. Press the Right Arrow key to move the blinking insertion point across the word *Memo*, and then press Home to move back to the beginning of the line. As you can see, navigating in a zoomed document is just like navigating in a document displayed at the default 100 percent size. You can also edit a zoomed document, though editing is not very practical at this percentage of reduction.

4. Click the Zoom button on the Power Bar and select 200% from the drop-down list to magnify your document.

5. Now try selecting a few of the other zoom options to see their effects, and then return the setting to 100%.

WordPerfect's views

WordPerfect's default viewing mode is Page, which shows all the elements of a document including margins, headers, and footnotes as they will appear on the printed page. (You can change the default by choosing Preferences from the File menu, clicking Display, selecting the View/Zoom option, and changing the Default View and Default Zoom settings.) You can see Page view at various levels of magnification by clicking the Zoom button on the Power Bar. Two Page view shows two full pages side by side. Draft view shows text and graphics as they will appear when printed but does not calculate page breaks or show page elements, such as headers and page numbers.

For documents that are more than one page long, you can view facing pages to ensure a pleasing presentation. Here's how:

Inserting page breaks

1. First simulate a two-page document by clicking an insertion point to the left of the *A* in *Attached* at the beginning of the second paragraph and pressing Ctrl+Enter to insert a page break at the insertion point.

Viewing facing pages

2. Choose Two Page from the View menu, and then press PgUp to display the memo as shown here:

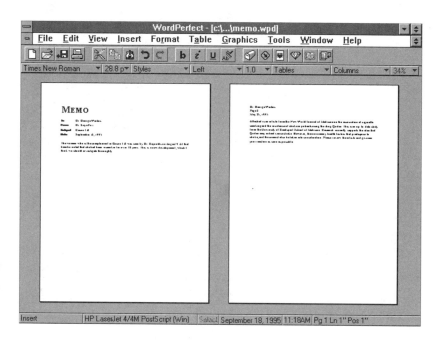

3. Point to the blank area below the text on the first page, click an insertion point at the end of the page, and press Delete to delete the page break. The second paragraph of the memo moves to the first page of the document, and the second page is now gray, indicating that it no longer exists.

4. Choose Page from the View menu to return to the familiar Page view.

Sending the File to the Printer

Now for the real test. Assuming that your printer is turned on and ready to go, follow along while we print the memo:

Faxing documents

If you have a fax modem, a fax driver, and a fax program that runs under Windows, you can fax documents from within WordPerfect for Windows. First select your fax driver in the Select Printer dialog box (see the tip on page 38). Then, in the Print dialog box, specify any other options you want, such as print selection and number of copies, and click the Print button. WordPerfect sends your document to your fax modem instead of to your printer.

The Print button

1. Click the Print button on the Toolbar to display the Print dialog box:

Take a moment to look over the options in the Print dialog box. You can control exactly how much of your document is printed by using the options in the Print Selection group box. You can also print a Document Summary (see the tip on page 76), and you can print a document directly from disk without loading it into WordPerfect. You can specify the number of copies to be printed, the print resolution, and whether to print graphics.

2. Be sure the Full Document option is selected in the Print Selection group box, and then click Print. WordPerfect sends the MEMO.WPD file to the printer, and printing begins.

If the printout of the memo doesn't look quite right, it's probably because your printer can't print some of the formatting used in the memo template. Otherwise, the printed memo should look like the one on page 27.

Now follow the steps below so that you can begin Chapter 3 with a clean document window:

1. Choose Close from the File menu.

2. When WordPerfect asks whether you want to save your changes, click Yes to save MEMO.WPD and clear the screen.

Mailing documents

If your system is set up to send and receive electronic mail using a standard protocol, the WordPerfect for Windows installation program detects your e-mail program. You can then mail a document from within WordPerfect by simply choosing the Send command from the File menu, making the usual settings, and then sending the file on its way. (If you have more than one e-mail program on your computer, a submenu will appear when you choose the Send command so that you can select the appropriate program.)

3

Fine-Tuning Your Documents: Creating a Business Letter

Adjust margins to balance the text on the page

Use borders and shading to emphasize paragraphs

Fox & Associates

Medical Malpractice Consultants

1224 Evergreen Road, Lake Oswego, OR 97035

September 21, 1995

Add interest with different types of justification

Mr. David Robertson
Sullivan, Duffy and Bridge, Attorneys at Law
145 Salmon Street
Portland, OR 97201

RE: CASE #312, REBECCA BRAND V. MIDVALLEY CLINIC

Dear Mr. Robertson:

Dr. George Winters and I have reviewed the medical files in the above case and have come to an opinion. We conclude that Rebecca Brand's stroke may have been exacerbated by her use of the drug Qnifen. However, in her case *other risk factors may have been equally or more important.*

Draw attention to important points by changing attributes

A number of case reports have associated stroke with Qnifen administration over several years. Patients taking Qnifen are frequently also taking many other drugs; however, the association of stroke with these drugs in the absence of Qnifen has not been documented.

The other risk factors that may also have played a role in Rebecca Brand's stroke are the following:

1. She is more than 59 years old.

2. She has smoked cigarettes for over 30 years.

3. She has mild hypertension.

Age, smoking, and hypertension are well-known risk factors for stroke.

Set off sections by changing indents and line spacing

I hope this summary of our opinion will be of help to you. Please call upon me for further information should you require it.

Sincerely,

Kaye E. Fox, Ph.D.

W hether you're writing letters for business or personal use, WordPerfect can simplify the entire process by making light work of tasks such as detecting and correcting spelling errors and adjusting margins. In this chapter, we build on what you learned in Chapter 2 to prepare a professional-looking letter. Let's get started:

1. Type the letter below, pressing the Enter key to add any necessary blank lines. (You can either type the entire letter or an abbreviated version, but to follow along, you must include the misspellings *reviewe*, *Qnifan*, and *mald*, the double words, and the mixed-up case in *pLease*. You must also include a numbered list.)

Fox & Associates
Medical Malpractice Consultants
1224 Evergreen Road
Lake Oswego, OR 97035

September 21, 1995

Mr. David Robertson
Sullivan, Duffy and Bridge, Attorneys at Law
145 Salmon Street
Portland, OR 97201

Re: Case #312, Rebecca Brand v. Midvalley Clinic

Dear Mr. Robertson:

Dr. George Winters and I have reviewe the medical files in the above case and have come to an opinion. We conclude that Rebecca Brand's stroke may have been exacerbated by her use of the drug Qnifan. However, in her case other risk factors may have been equally or more important.

A number of case reports have associated stroke with Qnifan administration over several years. Patients taking Qnifan are frequently also taking many other drugs; however, the the association of stroke with these drugs in the absence of Qnifan has not been documented.

The other risk factors that may also have played a role in Rebecca Brand's stroke are the following:

1. She is more than 59 years old.
2. She has smoked cigarettes for over 30 years.
3. She has mald hypertension.
Age, smoking, and hypertension are well-known risk factors for stroke.

I hope this summary of our opinion will be of help to you. Please call upon me for further information should you require it.

Sincerely,

Kaye E. Fox, Ph.D.

---

2. Save the letter as LETTER.WPD.

Before we go any further, notice that WordPerfect has already corrected the capitalization error in the word *pLease*. Word-Perfect's QuickCorrect feature, which is on by default, takes care of many common typing and spelling errors and can also be used to automate the entry of frequently used words or phrases. You'll learn more about QuickCorrect in Chapter 5.

QuickCorrect

Fine-Tuning the Letter's Contents

Before modifying the way any document looks, you should be sure it accurately says what you want it to say. If you spend time formatting a letter so that it fits on one page and then make major content changes, such as adding a sentence or two, your formatting efforts may be wasted. In this section, the changes you'll make are small, but they are significant in terms of the impression your letter will make on its readers. We show you how to use the powerful Find and Replace commands and then how to put the Speller program through its paces. With these features at your fingertips, you'll be able to mop up errors and fix inconsistencies in no time.

Finding and Replacing Text

With the Find And Replace command, you can move quickly to any location in a document by giving WordPerfect a word, phrase, or code to find (called a *search string*). You can also use this command to locate a specific word, phrase, or code and replace it with a new word, phrase, or code.

Let's use the Find And Replace command in the letter to locate the word *Qnifan*:

1. Press Ctrl+Home to be sure the insertion point is at the beginning of the letter.

2. Choose the Find And Replace command from the Edit menu to display the Find And Replace Text dialog box shown on the next page.

Find options

The Find And Replace Text dialog box provides several menus with commands for customizing searches. For example, if you choose the Whole Word command from the Match menu and then enter *cat* as the search string, WordPerfect will not stop on *category* or *catalog*. To perform a case-sensitive search, choose Case from the Match menu; then if you enter *Cat*, WordPerfect finds only *Cat* and not *cat*. To extend the selection from the insertion point to the search string, choose Extend Selection from the Action menu. To position the insertion point before or after the search string, choose the appropriate command from the Action menu.

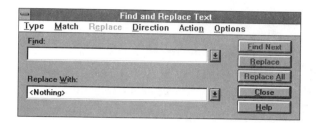

3. Type *Qnifan* in the Find edit box, and then click the Find Next button. WordPerfect instantly highlights the first occurrence of *Qnifan*.

4. Click the Find Next button to find the second occurrence of *Qnifan*.

Searching backward →

5. Choose Backward from the Direction menu at the top of the Find And Replace Text dialog box and then click the Find Prev button to move back to the first occurrence of *Qnifan*.

If you have been following along with previous examples, you know that the word *Qnifan* should actually be *Qnifen*. You can quickly correct this error by using the Find And Replace command, as follows:

1. With the Find and Replace Text dialog box still open, click an insertion point at the beginning of the first paragraph.

2. Click <Nothing> in the Replace With edit box, and then type *Qnifen*.

3. Choose Forward from the Direction menu, and click the Find Next button. WordPerfect highlights the first occurrence of the word *Qnifan*.

4. Click Replace. WordPerfect replaces the first *Qnifan* with *Qnifen* and moves to the second *Qnifan*.

5. Click Replace All. WordPerfect moves through the document, automatically replacing all the remaining occurrences of *Qnifan* with *Qnifen*.

6. When the replace operation is complete, click Close to close the dialog box and return to the document window.

7. Now with all four *Qnifens* in place, save the letter.

Finding or replacing codes

To find or replace codes, choose Codes from the Match menu of the Find And Replace Text dialog box. When the Codes dialog box appears, highlight the code you want to find or replace, and then click Insert to enter the code in the Find edit box. The Codes dialog box remains open so that you can enter another code in the Replace With edit box (or you can close the dialog box and replace the code with nothing). Then click Find Next or Replace to find or replace the code. To narrow the search for a specific code, choose Specific Codes from the Type menu, select a code, and then select the appropriate options in the resulting Find And Replace Text dialog box before clicking Find Next or Replace.

Checking Spelling

Nobody spells or types perfectly all the time. Fortunately, WordPerfect's Spell Checker program detects not only spelling errors but also double words and inappropriate capitalization. What's more, Spell Checker is so easy to use that you'll have no excuse for not spell-checking every WordPerfect document you create.

Spell Checker works by comparing the words in your document with the words in its dictionary. If Spell Checker can't find a matching word in its dictionary, it displays a list of alternative spellings. If the word is an error, you can correct it either by selecting a replacement word from Spell Checker's Suggestions list box or by editing the word yourself. If the word is not an error—for example, Spell Checker might stumble over obscure slang terms and some proper names, such as *Midvalley*—you can click the Skip Once button to tell Speller to ignore this instance of the word but stop for future instances, or you can click the Skip Always button to tell Spell Checker not to stop for that word again.

How Spell Checker works

Slang and proper names

With the letter displayed on your screen, follow these steps to check your spelling:

1. Move the insertion point to the beginning of the letter, and click the Spell Check button on the Toolbar. WordPerfect displays this dialog box:

The Spell Check button

2. Spell Checker has stopped on the name *Midvalley*. Click the Skip Always button to tell Spell Checker to ignore this and any other instances of that name in the document.

Spell-checking as you write

If you are unsure of the spelling of a word, simply highlight the word and click the Spell Check button. WordPerfect gives you instant feedback, enabling you to correct your work in progress.

3. Spell Checker stops on *reviewe*, displaying this list of possible replacements:

4. Select *reviewed* in the Suggestions list box, and then click the Replace button.

5. When Spell Checker stops on *Qnifen*, click Skip Always.

6. When Spell Checker stops on the double words *the the*, click Replace to delete the second *the*.

7. When Spell Checker stops on *mald*, double-click the suggested word *mad* in the Replace With edit box to select it, type *mild*, and click Replace.

Spell Checker displays a message box when the spell-check is complete. Click Yes to return to the document window, and then save your corrected letter.

Take the time to experiment with Spell Checker. The program is not infallible, but running it on important documents might save you from unpleasant typographical embarrassments.

Fine-Tuning the Letter's Appearance

The letter you've typed is fairly presentable, but you can do a lot to fine-tune its appearance. In this section, we show you how to format documents by applying attributes and changing the justification, line spacing, indentation, fonts, and margins.

Applying Attributes

You apply *attributes* to your text to dress it up and to emphasize certain words. WordPerfect allows you to apply the most

Supplementary dictionaries

WordPerfect attaches a supplementary dictionary to every document you create. If you want Spell Checker to ignore certain words when it spell-checks your document, you can add these words to the supplementary dictionary. To work with this dictionary or to create and edit your own supplementary dictionaries, choose Supplementary from Spell Checker's Dictionaries menu, and then add, edit, or delete words as necessary.

common attributes—bold, italic, and underlining—with just the click of a button. Try this:

1. Select the letter's subject line (the line that starts with *Re:*), and click the Bold button on the Toolbar.

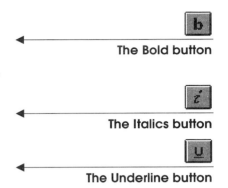

The Bold button

2. Select the words *other risk factors may have been equally or more important* at the end of the first paragraph, and click the Italics button on the Toolbar.

The Italics button

3. Select the line that begins with the word *Age* below the numbered list, and click the Underline button on the Toolbar. Here are the results:

The Underline button

Checking grammar

To catch errors of grammar, syntax, and improper word usage, use Word-Perfect's grammar-checker, Grammatik. This program applies common grammar rules to your text to identify potential problems, suggest corrections where appropriate, and provide helpful explanations if you request them. During a grammar-check, WordPerfect also spell-checks the document and accumulates statistics that assess the document's readability. To run Grammatik, press Ctrl+Home to move to the top of the document, and then choose Grammatik from the Tools menu. You can ignore "problems" you don't want to correct, implement suggested replacements, and make changes directly to your document without quitting Grammatik. When Grammatik finishes checking the document, you can save your changes to a custom writing style and view readability statistics.

Using the Thesaurus

WordPerfect's Thesaurus is a very handy way to find alternate words while writing documents. Simply select the word you want to change, and choose the Thesaurus command from the Tools menu. WordPerfect then displays a list of synonyms and antonyms for the selected word.

What else can we do to dress up the letter? Let's add weight to the subject line by making it uppercase. Here's how:

Capital letters →

1. Select the entire subject line, and choose Convert Case and then Uppercase from the Edit menu.

2. Click anywhere in the document to remove the selection so that you can see this result:

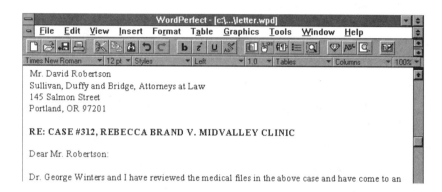

3. Once again, click the Save button to save the letter.

Justifying and Aligning Text

The way you justify and align your text affects the way it looks and can determine its impact. Generally, you justify multiple lines of text, and you align a single line.

The word *justification* means to arrange lines of text in such a way that all the lines come out even at one or both of the margins. WordPerfect offers five justification types: Left, Right, Center, Full, and All.

This is an example of left justification. These lines are even at the left margin and uneven (ragged) at the right margin. Justify letters this way when you want them to appear informal and friendly.

This is an example of right justification. These lines are even at the right margin and uneven at the left margin. This type of justification is rarely used in letters.

This is an example of center justification. These lines are centered between the left and right margins. Center justification is great for setting off multiple lines of text.

Other attributes

In addition to using Toolbar buttons to make the selected text bold, italic, or underlined, you can apply other appearance attributes, such as Redline, Strikeout, and Hidden, by choosing Font from the Format menu. Redline is often used to identify information that has been added to a document, and Strikeout can be used to identify suggested deletions. (These attributes are also used by the Compare Document feature to identify differences between one version of a document and another.) The Hidden attribute is often used for sensitive material you don't want displayed or printed. (To unhide the text, choose the Hidden Text command from the View menu.)

This is an example of full justification. The lines are even at both the right and left margins. Justify letters this way when you want them to appear formal and professional.

This is an example of all justification. The lines have been stretched to reach the left and right margins by adding space between the letters and words. This format is useful for banner headings.

When you start WordPerfect, left justification is the default, so if you print the letter now, the lines will be uneven at the right margin. If you want a different type of justification, you can change the setting before or after you type the document. Follow these steps to switch to full justification:

1. To change the justification for an entire document, the insertion point must be at the very beginning of the document, so press Ctrl+Home.

2. Point to the Justification button on the Power Bar (where the word *Left* appears), hold down the left mouse button to display a drop-down list of options, and select Full. The word *Full* now appears on the Justification button.

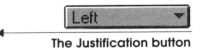

The Justification button

3. Scroll down to see how the letter looks with its new format, noticing that the lines are now even at both margins:

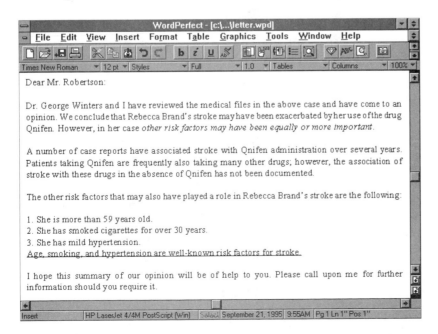

Now let's right-align the letter's date:

1. Click an insertion point to the left of the date, display the Justification button's drop-down list, and select Right. Oops! All the text from the insertion point on has moved to the right.

2. Click the Undo button to restore full justification so that we can try a different method.

Aligning one line → 3. With the insertion point still in front of the date, choose Line and then Flush Right from the Format menu. This time, only the date moves to the right:

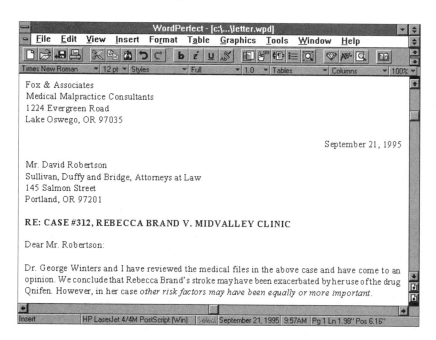

Now let's center the lines of the return address. Try these two methods:

1. Press Ctrl+Home to move to the top of the letter, and choose Line and then Center from the Format menu. The first line is now centered.

Aligning several lines → 2. Instead of center-aligning each of the remaining three lines individually, select the lines and then select Center from the Justification button's drop-down list. All three lines are centered at once.

To see an example of all-justified text, complete this step:

1. Select the entire subject line, and then select All from the Justification button's drop-down list. The line now stretches from the left to right margins, as shown here:

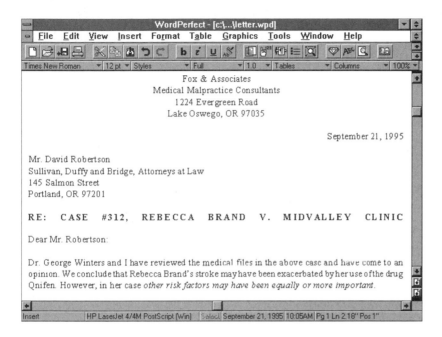

Taking a Look at WordPerfect's Codes

When you apply attributes, such as bold or italic, or change a document's justification or alignment, WordPerfect inserts codes in your document. These codes determine the way your document looks both on the screen and when printed. You cannot see the codes in the normal document window, but you can see them in WordPerfect's Reveal Codes area. By displaying this area, you can check the position of your formatting codes to be sure your document will appear on the printed page exactly the way you want it to.

To display the Reveal Codes area, follow these steps:

1. Press Ctrl+Home to move to the top of the letter, and choose Reveal Codes from the View menu. The screen splits in two, with the letter displayed in both parts, as you can see on the next page.

Realigning partial lines

You can choose Line and then Center or Flush Right from the Format menu to center or right-align part of a line of text. For example, if you type *Left*, choose Line and then Center, type *Center*, choose Line and then Flush Right, and type *Right*, the result looks like this:

Left   Center   Right

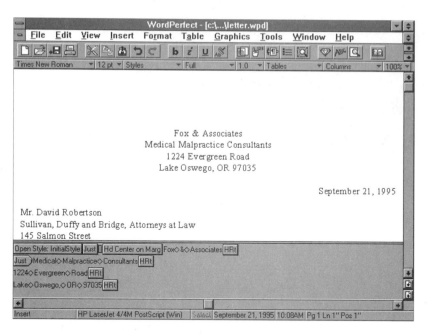

The normal document window occupies the top two-thirds of the screen, and the Reveal Codes area occupies the bottom one-third. You can move the insertion point, which is a solid block, around the Reveal Codes area just as you would move it around the document window.

The first code is Open Style: InitialStyle, which WordPerfect automatically inserts at the beginning of your documents. This code contains the information WordPerfect uses to control the general appearance of your documents. (We discuss initial codes on page 66.) The next code—Just—was added by WordPerfect when you changed the justification of the entire document to Full (see page 51).

2. Click the first Just code. It expands to Just: Full so that you can see the type of justification that is controlling the appearance of your document at that point. Full justification is in fact overridden by the next code—Hd Center on Marg, which means *force this line (Hd) to center between the left and right margins (Marg)*. WordPerfect inserted this alignment code when you chose Line and Center from the Format menu (see page 52).

3. Click the second Just code, which expands to Just: Center. This is where you changed the justification of the second,

Manipulating the Reveal Codes area

You can increase the size of the Reveal Codes area by first pointing to the top border of the area. Then when the mouse pointer changes to a double arrow, hold down the mouse button, and drag upward. Decrease the size by dragging downward. To quickly display the Reveal Codes area and adjust its size at the same time, point to the black bar above the up arrow on the vertical scroll bar, and drag downward, releasing the mouse button when the area is the size you want. Hide the area by dragging its top border downward off the screen.

third, and fourth lines of the return address to center justification (see page 52). Because you selected these lines, WordPerfect applied the justification change only to them by inserting a Just: Center code at the beginning of the selection to turn on center justification and a Just: Full code at the end to restore the full justification that you specified earlier for the entire document.

4. Examine the remaining codes in the Reveal Codes area by pressing the Down Arrow key. Notice particularly the "paired codes," such as Bold and Italc (for *Italic*). These codes have on and off components that tell WordPerfect when to turn the attribute on and when to turn it off.

Paired codes

Notice also the hard return (HRt) codes scattered throughout the letter. WordPerfect inserts these codes every time you press Enter. You'll also see soft return (SRt) codes, which indicate line breaks inserted by WordPerfect. They are called *soft returns* because their position changes as you edit the document.

Hard and soft return codes

5. Choose Reveal Codes from the View menu to close the Reveal Codes area.

Don't be intimidated by all the coding. If you're like most people, when you get used to the codes, you will think nothing of working in both the document window and the Reveal Codes area. You might even find editing and formatting documents in the Reveal Codes area just as easy as in the document window.

Adjusting Line Spacing

Usually, regular paragraphs in a letter are single-spaced, but sometimes you will want to change the spacing for specific elements, or you might want to specify double-spacing or even triple-spacing for drafts. WordPerfect's default line-spacing setting is 1.0—single-spacing. Changing this setting to 2.0 produces double-spacing, and changing it to 3.0 produces triple-spacing. You can enter numbers like 1.5 or 2.4 for more precise control. Follow the steps on the next page to double-space the numbered list in the letter.

Deleting formatting in the Reveal Codes area

Often the quickest way of turning off attributes and removing other types of formatting is to delete their codes in the Reveal Codes area. Simply move the insertion point before or after the code, and press Delete or Backspace to remove it. If the code is one of a pair, WordPerfect automatically removes the other code.

The Line Spacing button

1. Use the vertical scroll bar to scroll the numbered list into view, and click an insertion point to the left of the number 1.

2. Click the Line Spacing button on the Power Bar and select 2.0 from the drop-down list. Now all of the text from the numbered list to the bottom of the letter is double-spaced, as shown here:

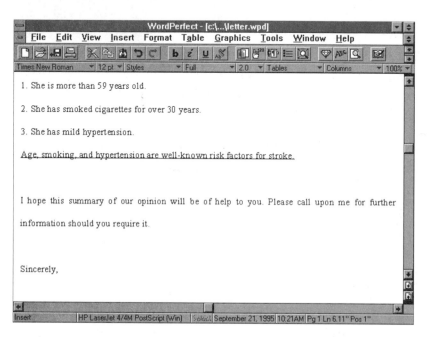

It's important to remember that when you add formatting to a document, you're also adding codes. The formatting remains in effect from the point in the document where a code turns it on to the point where another code turns it off. Because you want only the numbered list to be double-spaced, you must insert a code for single-spacing after the numbered list. Let's try a different method:

1. Click an insertion point to the left of *A* in *Age* (the first word following the numbered list), and choose Line and then Spacing from the Format menu to display this dialog box:

2. In the Spacing edit box, type *1* for single-spacing, and press Enter. (You can also click the arrows to the right of the edit box to adjust this setting up or down.) The lines following the numbered list are now single-spaced.

3. Choose Reveal Codes from the View menu to see the line spacing codes that WordPerfect has inserted in the letter. Choose Reveal Codes again to close the Reveal Codes area.

Indenting Paragraphs

The formatting we've added to the letter has improved its looks, but it could still use a touch or two. For example, we can indent the numbered list to make it stand out.

In WordPerfect, you can create several types of indents. You can indent whole paragraphs from just the left or from both the left and right; you can create hanging indents, where the second and subsequent lines of a paragraph are indented but the first line is not; and you can indent just the first line of a paragraph to more clearly separate it from the preceding one. How much you indent is a function of current tab settings. WordPerfect's default tab settings are at 1/2-inch intervals, but you can increase or decrease these intervals using the Tab Set command. (We talk more about setting tabs on page 108.) For now, we'll show you three simple techniques for indenting the numbered list in LETTER.WPD:

Types of indents

1. Click an insertion point in front of the 1 in the first line of the numbered list, and then click the Indent button on the Toolbar. (You'll have to click the down arrow at the right end of the Toolbar to scroll the Indent button into view.) WordPerfect indents the paragraph a half-inch.

The Indent button

2. Click an insertion point in front of the 2 in the second line of the list, and choose Paragraph and then Indent from the Format menu.

3. Now try a keyboard shortcut. Click an insertion point in front of the 3 in the third line, and press the F7 key. The results are shown on the next page.

Automatic code placement

You don't have to move the insertion point to the beginning of the paragraph before changing the format. WordPerfect automatically puts codes that control paragraph formatting, such as justification and line spacing, at the beginning of the paragraph containing the insertion point.

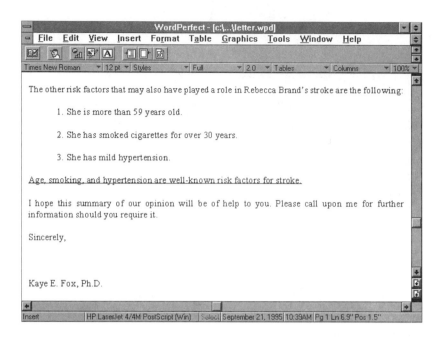

Changing the Font and Size

The appearance of your printed WordPerfect documents is a function of the fonts you use for your text. Which fonts you have available is determined by your printer. Most printers can print several fonts. WordPerfect 6.1 for Windows supports many fonts and provides internal font support so that you can view the fonts on your screen as they will appear when printed.

Fonts come in many shapes and sizes, but all fonts belong to one of two categories: *monospace* fonts (also known as *fixed pitch* fonts) and *proportional* fonts. Courier is an example of a monospace font. When you print a document in Courier, every character occupies the same amount of space. In other words, an *m* takes up the same amount of space as an *l*, as shown here:

```
mmmmmmmmmmmm
llllllllll
```

Times New Roman is an example of a proportional font, in which every character occupies an amount of space that is

---

First line indents (and outdents)

You can indent the first line of each new paragraph by choosing Paragraph and then Format from the Format menu and specifying the size of the indent as the First Line Indent setting. Specifying a negative First Line Indent setting, such as -0.5, creates a hanging indent, where the first line is outdented from the rest of the lines in the paragraph. (You can also create outdents by choosing Paragraph and then Back Tab from the Format menu.)

proportional to its width. So an *m* takes up much more space than an *l*, as shown here:

mmmmmmmmmm
lllllllll

The appearance of your documents is not only affected by the font you use but also by the font size. In general, fonts are measured in terms of their height—the distance from the bottom of *descenders* (the part of letters such as *p* that descend below the line) to the top of *ascenders* (the part of letters such as *h* that ascend above the line). The unit of measure is called a *point* (abbreviated *pt*), and 1 point equals 1/72 inch. Depending on the font, you will probably use sizes between 9 points and 13 points for ordinary text and larger sizes for titles and headings. (The text in this book is 12.5 points, and the headings are 16 points, 14 points, and 12 points.)

Font sizes

With older versions of most word processors, the default font was generally Courier 10 pt, which resembled the output of a typewriter. If you wanted a more professional look, you had to manually change the font and possibly its size. With WordPerfect 6.1 for Windows, the default font and size is Times New Roman 12 pt, which produces perfectly acceptable, businesslike results. However, you might want to change these defaults, either for an entire document or for selected elements. Try this:

1. Press Ctrl+Home to move to the top of your document, and click the Font Face button on the Power Bar to display a drop-down list of the fonts available for your printer, with Times New Roman, the current font, selected.

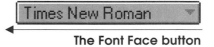

The Font Face button

2. Scroll the font list until you see Courier New. Then click Courier New to close the list and switch to that font.

3. Now change the size by clicking the Font Size button on the Power Bar and selecting 10 from the drop-down list of sizes. The results are shown on the next page.

The Font Size button

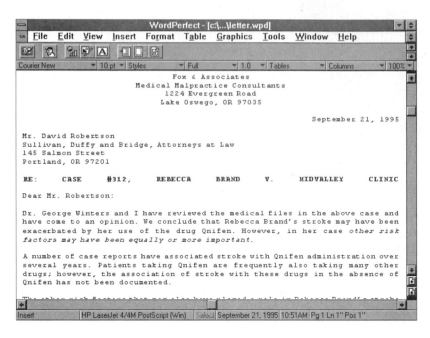

When you change a document's font or font size, the text might wrap differently than before.

4. The letter now looks pretty clunky. Use the Font Face and Font Size buttons to try a few other font and size combinations, and then return the letter to Times New Roman 12 pt.

Changing the font and size while the insertion point is at the top of the document affects the entire document. You can also make changes to just part of the document. Follow these steps:

1. Select the first line of the return address, and choose the Font command from the Format menu to display this dialog box:

Copying formatting

To quickly copy the formatting from one block of text to another, first select the formatted text, and click the QuickFormat button on the Toolbar or choose Quick-Format from the Format menu. When the QuickFormat dialog box appears, select the Characters option to copy only the font and other character attributes (bold, italic, and so on) or select the Headings option to copy Paragraph formatting too. Then simply drag the paint-roller pointer over the text you want to format. WordPerfect applies all the font and attribute formats of the selected text to the "painted" text. Click the QuickFormat button or choose the Quick-Format command again to stop "painting."

As you can see, the Font dialog box allows you to select a font and size, apply attributes, and change various other text characteristics all in one place. The box in the lower-left corner shows sample text as it would appear with your selections implemented.

2. Select 24 in the Font Size box, and click the Bold check box in the Appearance group box.

3. Click any font in the Font Face list and then use the Up and Down Arrow keys to scroll through the list, checking the sample box to see what each font will look like.When you have found a font that produces a strong look (we selected Swis721 BlkEx BT), click OK to return to the document window with your selections implemented.

4. Select the *F* in *Fox*, click the Font Size button on the Power Bar, and select 36. Repeat this step for the *A* in *Associates*.

Large first letters

5. Select the *Medical Malpractice Consultants* line, change the font size to 18 pt, and make the text italic. The return address now looks as shown here:

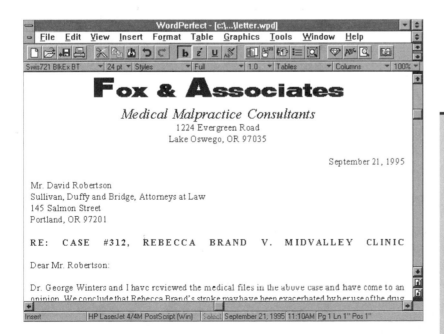

6. Save your work before moving on.

Other font options

In the Font dialog box, you can superscript or subscript selected text by using the options on the Position pop-up list, and you can select from a number of predetermined sizes, such as Large and Small, by using the options on the Relative Size pop-up list. You can also specify whether the Underline and Double Underline attributes should apply to spaces and tabs, and you can change the color and shading of the selected text in the Color Options group box.

Adding Borders and Shading

With WordPerfect 6.1 for Windows, you can add borders and shading to paragraphs with a few clicks of the mouse button. In this section, we'll add a border and shading to the return address at the top of the letter to give it the look of a letterhead. In the next chapter, we'll show you how to create even fancier letterheads. Follow these steps:

1. Select the four lines of the return address, and choose Paragraph and then Border/Fill from the Format menu to display this dialog box:

2. In the Border Options group box, click the down arrow at the right end of the Border Style option box, which currently contains *<None>*, and select Single from the drop-down list.

3. In the Fill Options group box, click the down arrow at the right end of the Fill Style options box, and select 20% Fill.

Visual border selection

To see the types of borders that result when you select border options from the Paragraph Border dialog box, you can click the box to the right of Border Style and then select from a palette of icons depicting the borders. If a border is almost, but not exactly, what you want, you can select it and then customize it by clicking the Customize Style button (see page 79 for more information).

4. Click OK. WordPerfect draws a border stretching from margin to margin around all four selected paragraphs and fills the space within the border with a 20 percent gray shading. (This gray shading is created with an even distribution of 20 percent black dots and 80 percent white dots. A 30 percent gray shading would be darker because it would have 30 percent black dots and 70 percent white dots, and a 10 percent shading would be lighter because the distribution would be 10 percent black and 90 percent white.)

5. To put a little more space between the last line of the return address and the bottom border, click an insertion point after

the *5* in the ZIP code, and press Enter. The border and shading grow to enclose the new blank line, and your screen now looks like this:

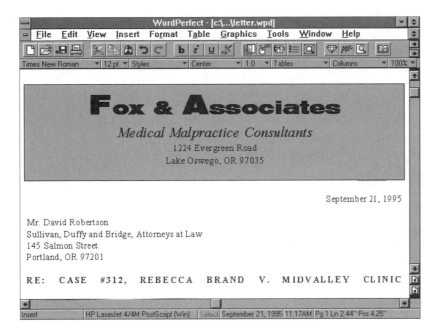

6. One more adjustment: The return address would look better if the address itself were on one line. It's easy to make this kind of edit in the Reveal Codes area, so choose Reveal Codes from the View menu, use the Arrow keys to move the insertion point to the left of the *L* in *Lake*, and press Backspace to delete the HRt code at the end of the preceding line. Now type a comma and a space, and choose the Reveal Codes command again to close the Reveal Codes area.

Setting Margins

One way to balance the proportions of a letter is to change its margins. WordPerfect's default left, right, top, and bottom margin settings are 1 inch. You might want to shorten a long letter by decreasing the left and right margins or lengthen a short letter by increasing those margins. You can also adjust the top and bottom margins to achieve the desired effect. Let's see what margin changes we can make to improve the positioning of the letter by following the steps on the next page.

Color shading

If you have a color printer or your documents are designed for screen presentation only, you might want to select a color for your fill patterns by clicking the icons to the right of the Foreground and Background options in the Paragraph Border dialog box and then selecting colors from the palettes to produce exciting visual effects.

1. Press Ctrl+Home to be sure the insertion point is at the beginning of the letter, and then click the Page/Zoom Full button on the Toolbar to see the entire page:

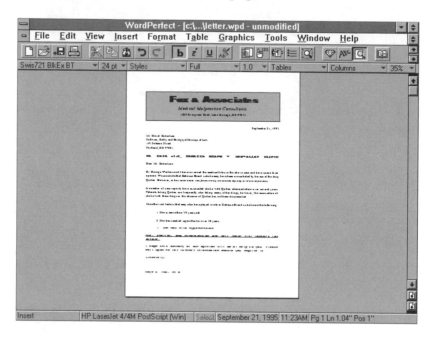

The letter sits a little low on the page, so let's move it up by decreasing the top margin and then increase the left and right margins so that the letter continues to occupy the full length of the page.

2. Scroll the Page Margins button into view on the Toolbar and then click the button to display the Margins dialog box:

3. Change both the Left and Right settings to *1.25*, change the Top setting to *0.5*, and click OK to return to the letter.

The Page Margins button

Displaying paragraph marks

As an alternative to working in the Reveal Codes area, you can display nonprinting characters such as paragraph marks, spaces, and tabs by choosing the Show ¶ command from the View menu. You can then delete characters such as paragraph marks without working "in the dark." Choose the command again to hide the characters.

Using the Page Margins button on the Toolbar (or the Margins command on the Format menu) changes the margins for the entire document. What if you want to adjust the margins for only one paragraph? Try this:

1. Select the entire subject line below the recipient's address, and choose Paragraph and then Format from the Format menu to display this dialog box:

Changing the margins of a paragraph

2. In the Paragraph Adjustments group box, click the upward-pointing arrowhead at the right end of the Left Margin Adjustment edit box until its setting is *0.700*.

3. Repeat step 2 for the Right Margin Adjustment setting, and click OK. Remove the highlight so that you can see the result, as shown here:

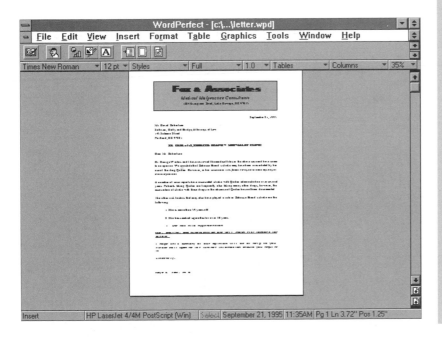

Centering vertically

Letters, particularly short ones, look best when they are centered on the page—that is, placed approximately the same distance from the top of the page as from the bottom. You could achieve this effect by adjusting your top and bottom margins, but Word-Perfect provides an easier way: Choose Page and then Center from the Format menu to display the Center Page(s) dialog box, select the Current Page option, and click OK. (If you want to center more than one page, you can select the Current And Subsequent Pages option instead; the insertion point must be located on the page where you want centering to begin.)

4. Click the Page/Zoom Full button to return to Page view, and then click the Save button to save the letter before continuing.

The new margin settings are controlled by the margin codes that you can see in the Reveal Codes area. (Click the codes to display their exact settings.) WordPerfect has put Top Mar, Lft Mar, and Rgt Mar codes at the top of the document, and beginning and ending Rgt Mar Adj (for *right margin adjustment*) and Lft Mar Adj codes around the subject line to limit your margin adjustments to that one paragraph.

Predefining Formats

As you work with WordPerfect, you might notice that you use some types of formatting for all your documents. For example, you might always use full justification. Instead of having to change the formatting every time you start a new document, you can predefine a format so that every document is full-justified. Let's experiment by predefining a format for the other documents you'll create in this book:

Initial codes

1. Choose Document and then Initial Codes Style from the Format menu to display the Styles Editor dialog box.

2. Choose Justification and then Full from the Style Editor's Format menu. A Just code appears in the Contents box.

3. Click the Just code. As in the Reveal Codes area, the code expands to Just: Full, like this:

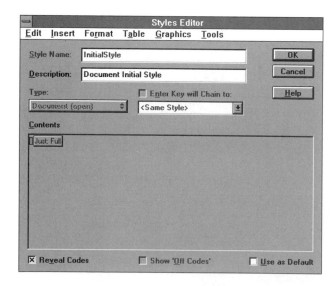

4. Click the Use As Default check box in the bottom-right corner of the dialog box to tell WordPerfect to apply this format to all future documents.

5. Click OK to return to the document window.

   From now on, every document you create in WordPerfect will be full-justified. If you want to change the justification of a particular document, you can still do so by placing the insertion point at the beginning of the document and making the necessary selection from the Format menu or the Power Bar.

Printing the Letter

Well, you now have an accurate, formatted letter ready for printing. Follow these steps:

1. Click the Page/Zoom Full button to check that all your formatting is in place. Then click Page/Zoom Full again.

2. Click the Print button on the Toolbar, and press Enter.

   Be sure to save the letter because you'll use it again in the next chapter when you create letterhead templates.

More About Templates:
Designing Great-Looking Letterheads

4

Fox & Associates

1224 Evergreen Road
Lake Oswego, OR 97035
(503) 555-4567
Fax: (503) 555-5678

October 4, 1995

Mr. David Robertson
Sullivan, Duffy and Bridge, Att
145 Salmon Street
Portland, OR 97201

Dear Dave:

Dr. George Winters and I hav
opinion. We conclude that R
drug Qnifen. However, in he
Please contact me for a summar

Sincerely,

Kaye E. Fox

Cc: Dr. George Winters

Fox & Associates
Medical Malpractice Consultants
1224 Evergreen Road Lake Oswego, OR 97035 (503) 555-4567

September 29, 1995

Mr. David Robertson
Sullivan, Duffy and Bridge, Attorneys at Law
145 Salmon Street
Portland, OR 97201

RE: CASE #312, REBECCA BRAND V. MIDVALLEY CLINIC

Dear Mr. Robertson:

Dr. George Winters and I have reviewed the medical files in the above case and have come to an opinion. We conclude that Rebecca Brand's stroke may have been exacerbated by her use of the drug Qnifen. However, in her case *other risk factors may have been equally or more important.*

A number of case reports have associated stroke with Qnifen administration over several years. Patients taking Qnifen are frequently also taking many other drugs; however, the association of stroke with these drugs in the absence of Qnifen has not been documented.

The other risk factors that may also have played a role in Rebecca Brand's stroke are the following:

1. She is more than 59 years old.

2. She has smoked cigarettes for over 30 years.

3. She has mild hypertension.

Age, smoking, and hypertension are well-known risk factors for stroke.

I hope this summary of our opinion will be of help to you. Plese call upon me for further information should you require it.

Sincerely,

Kaye E. Fox, Ph.D.

Most businesses use letterhead stationery. The advantage of using a computer-generated letterhead is that you don't have to switch the paper in your printer from plain bond to letterhead every time you print a letter. In this chapter, we'll show you how to use the Letter Expert and one of the WordPerfect letter templates that includes a letterhead. As you saw in Chapter 2, WordPerfect offers many different types of templates, from memos and letters to résumés and cash flow statements. We recommend that in addition to working through our examples, you take the time to explore WordPerfect's other templates on your own. You never know when one of them might be just right for the next document you plan to create.

When WordPerfect's templates don't quite meet your needs, you can always create your own. In the second half of this chapter, we'll introduce you to some new features so that you can create your own letterhead template. If you work for a company that already has preprinted letterhead, you probably have no choice about using it. However, you might want to use the instructions in this chapter to create a letterhead for your personal correspondence. As you follow along, you'll probably think of other ways you could put the letterhead techniques to work—for example, generating attractive flyers or eye-catching advertisements.

Using the Letter Expert

When you are learning to use WordPerfect or when you are in a hurry, the Letter Expert can help you quickly create a letter based on one of WordPerfect's letter templates. The Letter Expert walks you through the steps of writing a letter, asking for information and automating the process as much as possible. Assuming you're already in WordPerfect and your screen is clear, follow these steps to see the Letter Expert in action:

1. Click the New Document button on the Toolbar to display the New Document dialog box.

2. Next select Letter in the Group list, select <Letter Expert> in the Select Template list, and click the Select button. The Letter Expert displays this dialog box:

3. If necessary, select Contemporary Letterhead, and then click the Next button. The Letter Expert displays this dialog box so that you can enter the name and address of the person you are sending the letter to:

4. Before you enter the recipient information, click the Personal Info button, adjust the information in the dialog box that appears so that it looks as shown on the next page, and click Save As Default so that WordPerfect will use this information in all appropriate templates.

Editing the Personal Information

Enter Your Personal Information

Name:	Kaye E. Fox
Title:	
Organization:	Fox & Associates
Address:	1224 Evergreen Road
City, State ZIP:	Lake Oswego, OR 97035
Telephone:	(503) 555-4567
Fax:	(503) 555-5678

OK Cancel Next Field Save as Default Help

Entering addresses in the Address Book

Template Toolbar buttons

The buttons on the Toolbar (and the commands on some menus) change when you open a template so that you have direct access to the features you are most likely to use with that template. (You can use QuickTips to familiarize yourself with the buttons.) For example, the Toolbar buttons that appear when you open a letter template help simplify the task of creating a letter. You can readdress the current letter by clicking the Re-Address Letter button; or use one of Word-Perfect's ready-made letters, such as the formal invitation letter (INVITE.WPD), or a letter you've already written, by clicking the Insert Pre-Written Letter button. Other tasks you can perform with the Template Toolbar buttons include adding closings to letters and creating envelopes. When you use WordPerfect's templates, take advantage of the Template Toolbar buttons. They can really save you time.

5. Now for the recipient information. Instead of entering it directly in the Letter dialog box, click the Address Book button to display the Template Address Book dialog box, click Add, fill out the Edit Address dialog box as shown below, and click OK. (If Mr. David Robertson already appears in the Names box in the Template Address Book dialog box, click the Edit button, check that your information matches ours, and then click OK.)

Edit Address

Name:	Mr. David Robertson
Salutation:	Dear Dave
Title:	
Organization:	Sullivan, Duffy and Bridge, Attorneys
Address:	145 Salmon Street
City, State ZIP:	Portland, OR 97201
Telephone:	(503) 555-7653	Fax:	(503) 555-7654
Account/ID Number:	

OK Cancel Next Field Help

6. Back in the Template Address Book dialog box, click Add, fill out the Edit Address dialog box like this, and click OK:

Edit Address

Name:	Ms. Alannah Burke
Salutation:	Dear Alannah
Title:	
Organization:	Burke-Roney Law Offices
Address:	246 NE 42nd
City, State ZIP:	Seattle, WA 98117
Telephone:	(206) 555-9901	Fax:	(206) 555-3870
Account/ID Number:	

OK Cancel Next Field Help

WordPerfect adds this name and address to the Names list in the Template Address Book dialog box, which looks like this:

7. With Mr. David Robertson selected in the list, click the Select button to close the dialog box and add David Robertson's information to the Letter dialog box.

8. Click OK to close the Letter dialog box, read the next Letter Expert dialog box, and click Next so that you can write the text of the letter.

Instead of creating the letter's text from scratch, let's copy it from an existing document. Follow these steps:

1. Click the Open button, and double-click LETTER.WPD in the Open File dialog box to open the letter from Chapter 3.

2. Scroll the window until you can see the first paragraph, select it, and click the Copy button. Then close the letter.

3. Back in the new letter's window, click an insertion point below *Dear Dave*, and click the Paste button to insert the copied paragraph.

4. Select *above* in the first line, replace it with *Brand*, and then add the following sentence to the end of the paragraph:

Please contact me for a summary of our report.

Finally, we'll let the Letter Expert add the letter's closing:

1. Click the Continue button in the message box in the top-right corner of the document window. The Letter Expert displays the dialog box shown on the next page.

QuickList

Have you wondered about the QuickList option in several of WordPerfect's dialog boxes, such as Open File and Save As? You can set up QuickList so that you can quickly access the files and directories you use most often. Simply choose any command whose resulting dialog box offers the QuickList option, such as the Open command on the File menu. When the dialog box appears, click the QuickList option, and select Show QuickList to display the QuickList box in the active dialog box. Next select the Add Item option from the QuickList drop-down list, and enter a full pathname and description for the files or directories you want to include in the QuickList. When you use a dialog box that requires you to enter a filename or directory, you can then quickly select the file or directory from the Quick-List. If you want to redisplay the Directories list, select Show Directories or Show Both from the QuickList drop-down list. You can also edit and delete items in the QuickList by using the corresponding options in the QuickList drop-down list.

2. Click an insertion point in the Courtesy Copies To edit box, type *Dr. George Winters*, and click OK. The Letter Expert adds the closing information to the letter and displays this dialog box:

Watermarks

Watermarks are logos, graphics, or display type that appear "behind" the text of your document. (Diplomas and stock certificates often sport watermarks.) You can use WordPerfect's Watermark feature to create your own stationery or to dress up other documents. Choose Watermark from the Format menu, and click Create in the Watermark dialog box. (You can have up to two different watermarks—A and B—in a document.) Then use the Watermark Feature Bar as well as WordPerfect's commands and buttons to create a watermark. For example, click the Image button on the Watermark Feature Bar, and select one of Word-Perfect's graphics from the Insert Image dialog box. Then click Close on both the Graphics Box Feature Bar and the Watermark Feature Bar to return to the document window, where you can enter text. (For more information about graphics, see Chapter 6.)

3. Select only the Save and Print options, and then click the Finish button.

4. When the Letter Expert displays the Save As dialog box, type *letter2* as the filename, and click OK. The Letter Expert then sends the letter to the printer, and the results are shown on page 69.

5. Close the letter.

You might want to try out the other letter templates to see which one you like best. Then rejoin us for the next section, where we show you how to create a brand new template that you can add to WordPerfect's template library.

Creating a Letterhead from Scratch

The letterheads that come with WordPerfect's letter templates do the job, but they are very simple. Let's explore some of the WordPerfect features that can help you create a more sophisticated letterhead. As you follow along, refer to the letter shown at the beginning of the chapter so that you can see the effect you are aiming for.

To be able to use the new letterhead repeatedly, we must designate it as a template and assign it to a template group. Follow these steps:

1. Click the New Document button on the Toolbar. Then in the New Document dialog box, click the Options button, and select New Group.

   Creating a new template group

2. In the New Group dialog box, type *letterhd* in the New Group Name edit box, and click OK.

3. Back in the New Document dialog box, select Letterhd, click Options, and select New Template. WordPerfect opens a new template window and displays the Template Feature Bar below the Power Bar, like this:

   Creating a new template

Saving a Template

Working with a new template is just like working with a new document. Until you save the template, it exists only in your computer's memory. Follow the steps on the next page to save the template so that it is accessible through the New Document dialog box.

1. Choose Save As from the File menu to display the Save Template dialog box:

```
┌─────────────────────────────────────────────────┐
│ ▬              Save Template                      │
│                                                   │
│ Description:      ┌──────────────┐   ┌────────┐   │
│                   │              │   │   OK   │   │
│                   │              │   └────────┘   │
│                   │              │   ┌────────┐   │
│                   │              │   │ Cancel │   │
│ Template Name:    ┌──────────┐   │   └────────┘   │
│                   │          │       ┌────────┐   │
│                   └──────────┘       │  Help  │   │
│ Template Group:   ┌──────────────┐▲  └────────┘   │
│                   │ calendar     │                │
│                   │ envelope     │                │
│                   │ fax          │                │
│                   │ legal        │                │
│                   │ letter       │                │
│                   │ letterhd     │                │
│                   │ main         │▼                │
│                   └──────────────┘                │
└─────────────────────────────────────────────────┘
```

2. In the Description edit box, type *Fox & Associates - with border and vertical box*, and press Tab.

3. In the Template Name edit box, type *f&a*, and click OK. WordPerfect adds the extension WPT to identify this file as a template.

Putting a Border Around the Page

Now we can lay the groundwork for the new letterhead. The first step is to create the border that appears around the perimeter of the page:

1. Decrease all four margins by choosing Margins from the Format menu and setting the Left, Right, Top, and Bottom margins to *0.25*.

2. Choose Page and then Border/Fill from the Format menu to display the Page Border dialog box, which is similar to the Paragraph Border dialog box shown on page 62. Select Hairline from the Border Style drop-down list, and click OK. (You can click the sample box to the left of the Border Style option box to display samples of all the available border styles with the current selection highlighted.)

Inserting a Text Box

Now we need to insert a text box that will contain the text of the letterhead. As its name implies, a text box contains an

---

Document summaries

You can attach a document summary to your document by choosing Document Summary from the File menu and filling in the appropriate information in the Document Summary dialog box. You can enter general information about your document, such as a descriptive name, author, subject, and so on, that you can use later to help organize and locate the document file (see the tip about QuickFinder on page 37). Use the Configure and Options buttons in the Document Summary dialog box to change the summary fields, extract information from the document, and print, delete, or save the summary as a separate document. You can automatically attach summaries to all your documents by choosing Preferences from the Edit menu, double-clicking the Summary icon in the Preferences dialog box, and selecting Create Summary On Save/Exit.

insertion point so that you can enter and format text directly in it. Follow these steps:

1. Scroll the Toolbar, and click the Text Box button. Word-Perfect inserts a text box that looks like this:

The Text Box button

The text box is surrounded by small black squares, called *handles*, to indicate that it is active. The title bar indicates that the Text Box Editor is currently active. You can move around the Text Box Editor just as you move around the normal document window, and you can use many of the same menu commands and buttons. Notice that WordPerfect has replaced the Template Feature Bar with the Graphics Box Feature Bar. As you'll see, you can use the Graphics Box Bar to manipulate text boxes in various ways. (In Chapter 6, you'll use the buttons on this feature bar to work with graphics.)

Handles

2. In the text box, type *Fox & Associates*, and press Enter. On the second line, type *Medical Malpractice Consultants*, and press Enter.

Entering text in a text box

3. Type the last line of the letterhead, *1224 Evergreen Road Lake Oswego, OR 97035 (503) 555-4567*, inserting two spaces between *Evergreen Road* and *Lake Oswego* and between the ZIP code and the telephone number. Don't worry about bad breaks or strange word spacing; we'll take care of that later.

Colorific!

WordPerfect offers a whole host of colors that can be used for text, borders, fill, and anything else that appears in the document window. All you have to do is click the Color box in dialog boxes, such as the Font and Customize Border dialog boxes, and select a color from the available color palette. Even if you don't have a color printer, it's fun to experiment with the color palette. And if you're not satisfied with the current palette, you can change to a different one or create your own. Choose Font from the Format menu, and click the Palette option at the bottom of the Font dialog box to display the Define Color Printing Palette dialog box. Click the Open button to select a different palette or use the color wheel and color models to define a new palette. You can use the options below the color palette to change the palette's size, to copy a color and paste it over another, to invert the selected color, to blend colors, or to create a spectrum of colors. After you've defined your color palette, click Save As, and give your palette a name. You can return to the default palette by clicking the Default option. Finally, you can display the colors in the color palette in list form by selecting the Show As List option at the top of the dialog box. (You can even assign names to the colors in the list by selecting a color and then entering a name for it in the Name edit box.)

4. Click the Position button on the Graphics Box Bar to display this dialog box:

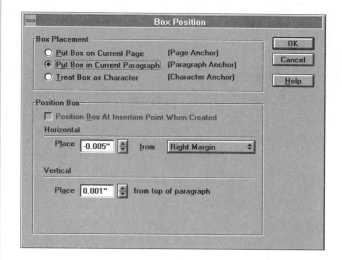

5. Select the Put Box On Current Page option, and click OK. Now the text box is anchored to the page rather than attached to the first paragraph of the template.

Before we go any further, here are a few pointers about working with text boxes and the Text Box Editor:

- To deactivate the Text Box Editor, click anywhere outside the currently selected text box.

- To activate the Text Box Editor, double-click anywhere inside the text box.

- To choose the commands that are applicable to text boxes, right-click the text box to display its QuickMenu.

- To remove the Graphics Box Bar, click its Close button.

- To display the Graphics Box Bar, right-click the text box, and choose Feature Bar from the QuickMenu.

With that out of the way, let's concentrate on changing the text box's size and adding a border:

1. Be sure the Text Box Editor is still active (check the title bar, and double-click the text box if it's not active). Then click the

Size button on the Graphics Box Bar to display the Box Size
dialog box shown here:

2. Change the Width setting by double-clicking the current
setting in the Set edit box and typing *1.35*.

3. Change the Height setting by simply selecting the Full option
(for *full page*). Then click OK to return to the Text Box Editor.

Now we'll add a border so that the text box is easier to see:

1. Click the Border/Fill button on the Graphics Box Bar to display the Box Border/Fill Styles dialog box, and select Hairline
from the Border Style drop-down list.

Adding a border to
a text box

2. Next click the Customize Style button to display the dialog
box shown here:

You can use the Customize Border dialog box to change the entire border or specific sides of the border, to change the color of the border (see the tip on page 78), to round the corners, and to add a drop shadow (both discussed on page 144). We'll use this dialog box to add a little buffer space between the letterhead and any letters that we merge later.

Adding a buffer space

3. Double-click the setting in the Outside Space edit box, and type *0.2*. Then click OK twice to return to the Text Box Editor.

Now let's reposition the text box on the page:

1. Point to the text box's border (away from the handles), and when the pointer changes to a four-headed arrow, hold down the mouse button, and drag the text box to the left side of the page, as far as it will go.

2. Fine-tune the text box's position by clicking the Position button on the Graphics Box Bar, typing *6.70* in the Horizontal Place edit box and *0* in the Vertical Place edit box, and clicking OK. Then click anywhere outside the text box to deactivate the Text Box Editor.

As you continue to work with WordPerfect's text box and graphics features, you'll find that you often have to make several adjustments to achieve the right effect. For example, now that we've repositioned the text box, it no longer fits neatly inside the page border. Resize the text box manually by following these steps:

1. If necessary, scroll to the top of the document window, and click the text box once to select it. (Notice that when the text box is selected in the document window, WordPerfect dims many of the commands and buttons, indicating that they cannot be used.)

2. Point to any handle at the top of the text box, and when the pointer changes to a double-headed arrow, drag the handle until the dotted border representing the text box aligns with the top of the page border.

3. Repeat step 2 for the bottom of the text box, and then click the document window to deselect the text box.

Adding prompts

You can use the Build Prompts button on the Template Feature Bar to add prompts to a new template. When you open a template that includes prompts, the Template Information dialog box appears, requesting that you fill in the information specified by the prompts. The information is then inserted in the template. To add a prompt, first click an insertion point in the template you are creating, and then click the Build Prompts button on the Template Feature Bar. When the Prompt Builder dialog box appears, click Add, and then type a name, such as *Date*, for the prompt and click OK. Back in the Prompt Builder dialog box, click the Paste button, and then click OK. WordPerfect displays a message box to inform you that it is running the Prompts macro. Then you are returned to the document window, where the prompt has been inserted in square brackets in the template. When you open the template for use later, the Template Information dialog box is displayed so that you can enter the information, such as the date, specified by the prompt.

Next we'll do something about the letterhead text. First we'll move it to the top of the text box and rotate it 90 degrees counter-clockwise. Then we'll add a little formatting, like this:

1. Double-click the text box to activate the Text Box Editor, and then click the Content button on the Graphics Box Bar to display the dialog box shown here:

Repositioning and rotating text in a text box

Note that you can use the Filename edit box in the Box Content dialog box to insert an existing text file into the selected text box.

2. Point to the arrows at the right end of the Vertical Position edit box, and select Top from the pop-up list. Then select 90 Degrees from the Rotate Contents Counterclockwise group box.

3. Click the Edit button to return to the Text Box Editor. Because you have rotated the text, the Text Box Editor displays the text in a special window like this:

Editing rotated text

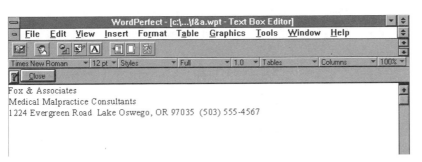

Formatting the
letterhead text

4. With the insertion point at the beginning of the text, select Right from the Justification drop-down list on the Power Bar.

5. Without moving the insertion point, choose Font from the Format menu, select Humanst521 Cn BT, click Bold in the Font Style list, select 36 from the Font Size list, and click OK.

6. Then move the insertion point to the beginning of the second line of the letterhead, and select 18 from the Font Size drop-down list on the Power Bar.

7. Click the Close button to return to the document window, and then press Ctrl+Home. The letterhead now looks like this:

TextArt

If you want to add a touch of whimsy to your letterhead, or if you need a special artsy look for a brochure or flyer, try Word-Perfect's TextArt feature, which enables you to create special effects with text. Click the TextArt button on the Toolbar to display the TextArt window. Then type your text, and select a shape to "pour" the text into. You can specify a text color, a shadow weight and pattern, an outline weight and color, and a fill pattern by clicking their respective buttons and selecting from the available options. You can also specify the angle of rotation and font and style of the text. When the text in the sample box looks the way you want it, click anywhere outside the TextArt box to return to your document with the text in place. To edit the text after embedding, double-click it to redisplay it in the TextArt window, where you can adjust it to your heart's content.

8. Save the letterhead by clicking the Save button on the toolbar. (You may have to scroll the button into view.)

The text of the letterhead and the top border of the text box are a little too close for comfort. We can easily correct this problem by increasing the right margin. (Yes, the *right* margin, not the *top* margin. Because we rotated the text 90 degrees counterclockwise, what appears to be the top margin is actually the right margin.) Follow the steps on the facing page to make the margin adjustment.

1. Double-click the text box to activate the Text Box Editor.

Adjusting the text box margins

2. With the insertion point at the beginning of the letterhead, choose Margins from the Format menu.

3. In the Margins dialog box, type *0.5* in the Right edit box, and click OK. Then click the Close button to return to the document window.

WordPerfect not only offers you a wide range of choices for putting borders around text, but as you saw in Chapter 3, you can also fill the space between borders with a variety of patterns or shading. Let's finish up this letterhead by adding a fill pattern to the text box:

1. Click the text box once, and then click the Border/Fill button on the Graphics Box Bar.

Adding a fill pattern

2. In the Box Border/Fill Styles dialog box, select Diagonal Lines 1 from the Fill Style drop-down list.

3. Click the Foreground option to display a color palette, and select the light gray color (ninth from the left).

4. Click OK to return to the document window. You can see the result in the illustration at the beginning of the chapter.

5. Click Close to remove the Graphics Box Bar.

Inserting a Date Code

Before moving on to the next section, let's insert a Date code at the top of the letterhead. When you include a Date code in a document, WordPerfect automatically inserts the current date (from your system clock) at the location of the code every time you load or print the document. Follow these steps:

1. Click an insertion point at the top of the document, choose Date and Date Code from the Insert menu, and press Enter.

2. Save the letterhead template by clicking the Exit Template button on the Template Bar. When WordPerfect asks whether you want to save your changes, click Yes.

If your letterhead doesn't print correctly

We've included several elements in the letterhead to show you some of the possibilities. If your printed letterhead doesn't look like ours, it may be that your printer can't handle some of these elements. For example, our HP LaserJet 4M prints the complete page border and the diagonal text-box fill at 600 dpi but not at 300 dpi. You may need to experiment with other border and fill options to create a letterhead your printer can print correctly.

Using the New Template

After you have created a template, you use it the same way you use WordPerfect's built-in templates. Follow these steps to create a letter based on the Fox & Associates template:

1. Open a new document based on the F&A.WPT template by clicking the New Document button on the Toolbar, selecting the Letterhd group, and then double-clicking Fox & Associates in the Select Template list box.

2. Click the Open button on the Toolbar, and then double-click LETTER.WPD to open the letter file.

3. Click an insertion point to the left of the *M* in *Mr. David Robertson*, and then press Shift+Ctrl+End to select all of the text from the insertion point to the end of the document.

4. Click the Copy button on the Toolbar, and then close the LETTER.WPD file. In the Document2 window, press Ctrl+End, and then press Enter twice to add some space.

5. Next click the Paste button on the Toolbar to place the copy of the letter at the insertion point in the letterhead template.

6. Save the merged document with the name *letter3* and press Ctrl+Home. Your screen now looks like this:

Inserting files

In addition to cutting and pasting, you can use the File command on the Insert menu or the Insert File button on the Template Feature Bar to insert one document into another. First click an insertion point in the current document, and choose File from the Insert menu. When the Insert File dialog box appears, select the name of the file you want to insert, and click the Insert button. If WordPerfect asks whether you want to insert the file into the current document, click Yes. Easy as pie.

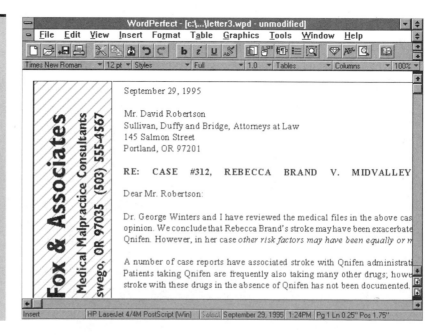

Notice anything wrong? The margins of the letter have changed to reflect the current setting for the letterhead, which is 0.25 inch for the left, right, top, and bottom margins. Here's how to fix this problem:

1. Select the text of the letter, excluding the date.

2. Click the Paragraph Format button on the Toolbar to display the Paragraph Format dialog box (see page 65). Type *1* in the Right Margin Adjustment edit box, and click OK.

3. Now move the text down from the top of the page. Click an insertion point to the left of the date, and choose Typesetting and then Advance from the Format menu to display this dialog box:

← The Paragraph Format button

4. Select the Down From Insertion Point option, type *1* in the Vertical Distance edit box, and click OK.

5. Print the document, which should be identical to the letter at the beginning of the chapter. Then choose Close from the File menu, and when WordPerfect asks if you want to save your changes, click Yes.

Creating a Directory for Letters

Without leaving WordPerfect, you can organize your files by creating directories for specific types of documents and then moving or copying your files to the new directories. For

File management

In several dialog boxes, you can use the options available in the File Options drop-down list to copy and move files to other directories, rename and delete files, print the current file list, and remove and rename an existing directory. You can even change the status of a file's "protective attributes" by selecting Change Attributes from the File Options drop-down list, and then selecting or deselecting the appropriate attributes. (Archive tells third-party backup programs that the file has changed since the last backup; Read-Only protects the file from deletion or modification; Hidden hides the file in dialog box file lists and in the Quick-Finder Search Results list; and System designates the file as part of your computer's operating system.) In addition, several dialog boxes have a Setup option you can use to change the display of files in the file list or to sort the list by filename, extension, size, date and time of creation, or descriptive name or type. (You can add a descriptive name and type in the Document Summary dialog box; see the tip on page 76.)

example, you can create a directory called *LETTERS* for your letters. (Directory names must be eight or fewer characters.) Take a few minutes to do that now:

1. Click the Open button on the Toolbar.

2. In the Open File dialog box, click File Options, and select Create Directory. WordPerfect displays this dialog box:

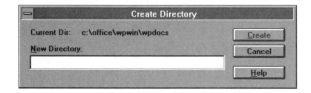

3. Type the full pathname of the new directory in the New Directory edit box (we typed *c:\office\wpwin\wpdocs\letters*), and click Create. The new directory appears as a subdirectory of WPDOCS in the Directories list box.

Now move the letter files:

Moving files to a new directory

1. Select the LETTER.WPD file, and then select Move from the File Options drop-down list to display this dialog box:

2. In the To edit box, type the pathname of the file in its new directory (we typed *c:*\office\wpwin\wpdocs*letters\letter.wpd*). You can also edit the existing pathname in the To edit box by clicking an insertion point after *wpdocs* and typing *letters*. Then click the Move button to move the file.

3. Now repeat steps 1 and 2 to move first LETTER2.WPD and then LETTER3.WPD.

Displaying files in a directory

4. To be sure that the letter files really were moved to the new directory, double-click the LETTERS directory in the Directories list box. Here they are:

5. Now double-click WPDOCS in the Directories list box to return to that directory, and then click Cancel to close the Open File dialog box.

That's all there is to creating directories!

5

More Advanced Techniques:
Creating a Professional Report

DRUG-INDUCED STROKE

Risk Factors

A number of important health
in humans. These include:

Age: The incidence of stroke
in young individuals. A sharp
of age.

Smoking: Smoking is a well
the more they have smoked, t
cessation of smoking at any ti
of coronary disease and heart
but in all likelihood the same

Hypertension: The risk of
elevated blood pressure. It has
is a major factor in reducing
pressure is diagnosed and tre

Diabetes: Diabetes and so
incidence of stroke. Diabetics
stroke. Whether strict contro
possible) reduces the risk of
progress.

Drugs

Three classes of drugs used th
with stroke.

Drugs That Stimulate
amphetamines, and cocaine.
amphetamines and cocaine ar
of all these drugs are:

- Increase blood pre
- Increase heart rate
- Stimulate brain

Fox & Associates   *Drug-Induced Stroke*

Drugs That Damage Blood Vessels: A few drugs used for long periods of time can damage blood vessels, which weakens their walls and, in the case of arteries in the brain, may lead to stroke. How these drugs produce this effect is not clear, but it is thought that it occurs in the following steps:

1. With continual administration over long periods of time, the drug accumulates in the cells that line the artery.

2. As the drug accumulates, it gradually inhibits the cells' metabolic processes.

3. Eventually the cells of the artery die, leaving the vessel wall weakened and vulnerable.

Qnifen and Fiszol: Both of these drugs are used to treat osteoporosis (softening of the bone). Both have also been associated with stroke, but to varying degrees. A summary description of the drugs is given below:

Qnifen was the first drug developed for the treatment of osteoporosis. However, after several years of use, it became associated with stroke.

Fiszol was recently approved for the treatment of osteoporosis. Because Fiszol has a different structure than Qnifen, current theory is that Fiszol will not have the same side effects. However, clinical trials have not yet corroborated this theory.

Although both Qnifen and Fiszol appear to be equally effective in treating osteoporosis, they differ greatly in their chemical structures. While Qnifen contains one methyl group (CH_3), Fiszol has none. This structural difference may explain why patients taking Qnifen have a higher incidence of stroke than patients taking Fiszol. The following statement was recently published in the *New World Journal of Medicine*:

Early reports of fewer cases of stroke associated with Fiszol would indicate that at this time, Fiszol is a better choice than Qnifen in the treatment of osteoporosis.[1]

---

[1]R. Urban, "Fiszol versus Qnifen and Stroke." New World Journal of Medicine, 217:312-315, 1995.

In many professions, writing reports is a common task. Whether you're a scientist, an administrative assistant, a marketing specialist, or an attorney, WordPerfect for Windows can help take the drudgery out of report writing. In this chapter, we'll introduce you to WordPerfect's features for creating outlines, styles, lists, parallel columns, and footnotes. In addition, we'll show you how to add headers and numbers to your pages.

To demonstrate these features, we need to work with a document that is longer than those we created in previous chapters. You can either create a report of your own or use the one shown on the previous page. In the following sections, you type just enough text to use the feature we are discussing. You can refer to the illustrations on the previous page to see how all these features can be combined to create a useful report.

Outlining Documents

Different people work in different ways. Some people launch right into a project, starting at the beginning and working their way through in a linear fashion until they've crossed the last *t* and dotted the last *i*. Others depend heavily on outlines, creating an overview of the project and then filling in the details. If you fall into the latter category, this section is for you. Although the report we're writing is relatively short, it contains enough headings to give you a good idea of how WordPerfect's Outline feature works. Follow these steps to see how easy it is to create an outline in WordPerfect:

The Outline Feature Bar →

1. With a clear document window, choose the Outline command from the Tools menu. As you can see at the top of the facing page, WordPerfect turns on the Outline Feature Bar, inserts a 1 followed by a period and a tab, and indicates that this is a first level heading by displaying a hollow 1 to the left of the number (you may have to scroll the window to see it). For good measure, WordPerfect also displays *Level 1* in the status bar and on the Select Style button of the Power Bar.

The Outline Definition button

2. Click the down arrow to the right of the word *Paragraph* on the Outline Bar, and select Outline from the drop-down list of available outline styles. WordPerfect changes the 1 to a Roman numeral I.

3. Choose Reveal Codes from the View menu. In the Reveal Codes area, notice that WordPerfect has inserted an Outline code, a Para Style code, and a Style code at the beginning of the document. Every time you press Enter while creating an outline, WordPerfect inserts a Para Style code after the hard return to identify the outline level and a Style code to control the numbering system. Choose Reveal Codes again to close the Reveal Codes area.

Now create the outline, using the Backspace or Delete key if you make a mistake:

1. Press the Caps Lock key, type *DRUG-INDUCED STROKE*, and then press Enter to start a new entry. WordPerfect inserts II at the beginning of the line.

2. Press the Tab key to change to level two. The insertion point moves over one tab, A replaces II, the level indicator to the left changes to a hollow 2, and the level 1 indicator for the preceding line acquires a minus (-) sign to indicate that it has sublevels. Press the Caps Lock key to turn off capitalization,

Report templates

Rather than create a report from scratch, you can tap into one of WordPerfect's report templates. (See page 28 for information on using templates.) These templates come with a number of report elements already formatted such as the title, headings, and page numbers. You can also use the buttons that appear on the Toolbar to simplify tasks such as generating a table of contents or creating a footnote.

type *Drugs*, and press Enter to start a new line. WordPerfect inserts B at the beginning of the line.

3. Press Tab to change to level three. The insertion point moves over one more tab, 1 replaces B, the level indicator changes to a hollow 3, and the preceding level 2 indicator acquires a minus sign.

4. Type *Drugs That Stimulate Blood Pressure:* (be sure to include the colon), and press Enter to start a new line. WordPerfect inserts a 2 at the beginning of the line.

5. Type *Drugs That Damage Blood Vessels:*, and press Enter.

6. Press Shift+Tab to change from level three to level two. The insertion point moves back one tab, B replaces 3, and the level indicator changes to 2. Type *Qnifen and Fiszol*, and press Enter to start a new line.

7. Type *Risk Factors,* and press Enter again to start a new line.

8. Press Tab to change to level three, and type four more entries for *Age:*, *Smoking:*, *Hypertension:*, and *Diabetes:*, but don't press Enter after *Diabetes*.

The Options button

9. Now click the Options button on the Outline Bar, and select End Outline to turn off outlining. (Notice that WordPerfect automatically inserts another line in your document, designating it with a T for *text*.) The outline now looks like this:

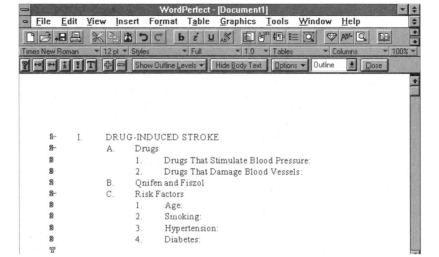

10. Choose Save As from the File menu, and save the outline in the C:\OFFICE\WPWIN\WPDOCS directory with the filename *report*. Then click the Print button on the Toolbar, and print the outline.

Viewing and Editing Outlines

Outlines are great for organizing your thoughts. It is a rare person who can create a perfect outline right off the bat, and most people have to spend some time organizing and reorganizing topics. WordPerfect's Outline feature enables you to see the structure of documents at any level of detail you choose, and it lets you move things around to your heart's content, searching for the most logical order. Let's take a brief look at some of these capabilities:

1. Move the insertion point to the beginning of the outline, click the Show Outline Levels button on the Outline Bar, and select 2 from the drop-down list to display only the level one and level two entries, like this:

The Show Outline Levels button

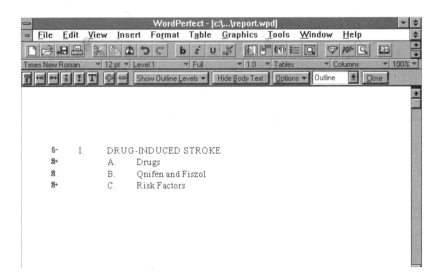

2. Move the insertion point to the first second-level entry (*Drugs*), and click the Show Family button on the Outline Bar to redisplay the level three entries under *Drugs*. (A *family* is an entry and its subentries.)

The Show Family button

The Hide Family button

The Next Level and Previous Level buttons

3. Repeat step 2 for the *Risk Factors* entry. (To once again hide these entries, you can simply click the Hide Family button on the Outline Bar.)

4. Move the insertion point to the *Qnifen and Fiszol* entry, and on the Outline Bar, click the Next Level button to change the entry level from two to three. (Clicking the Previous Level button—the one with the left-pointing arrow—does the opposite.) Notice that *Risk Factors* is renumbered from C to B.

5. Press the End key, and type a colon to make the *Qnifen and Fiszol* entry consistent with the other third level entries.

Now for a little rearranging:

Selecting a family

1. Click the 2 indicator to the left of the *Risk Factors* entry to select the entire family (the *Risk Factors* entry and all its subentries).

Moving a family

2. Point to the family's 2 indicator. When the pointer changes to a double-headed arrow, hold down the left mouse button, and drag upward until the line indicator is above the *Drugs* entry. When you release the mouse button, WordPerfect moves the *Risk Factors* family and automatically renumbers the outline entries, as shown here:

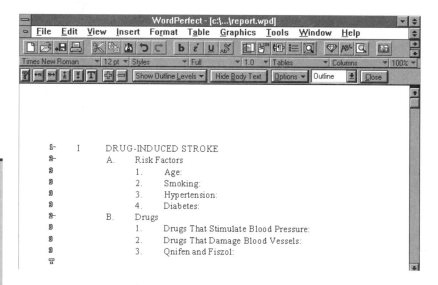

Moving entries with buttons

After selecting an entry or a family, you can move it up or down in the outline by clicking the Move Up and Move Down buttons (the buttons with the up and down arrows) on the Outline Feature Bar.

Let's add a little text to the outline:

1. Move the insertion point to the end of the *Risk Factors* entry, and then press Enter. WordPerfect creates another level two entry, labeled B.

2. For the new entry, type the following:

   A number of important health conditions are now recognized as contributing to the cause of stroke in humans. These include:

3. With the insertion point located at the end of the new text, click the Body Text button on the Outline Bar to change the entry to normal body text. (If you click the Next Level or Previous Level button on the Outline Bar, the text reverts to an outline level.)

The Body Text button

4. Press Enter to add a blank line below the text, and then move the insertion point to the end of the *Drugs* entry.

5. Press Enter, and type the following:

   Three classes of drugs used therapeutically or abused by drug-dependent individuals are associated with stroke.

6. Repeat step 3, and then press Enter to add a blank line.

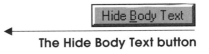

The Hide Body Text button

7. Click the Hide Body Text button on the Outline Bar to hide the outline's body text. Then to restore the text, click the Show Body Text button.

Converting Outlines to Documents

We need to get moving on the report, so follow these steps to change the entire outline to normal body text:

1. Press Ctrl+Home to move the insertion point to the top of the outline.

2. Choose Select and then All from the Edit menu to select the entire outline (including the body text), and then click the Body Text button on the Outline Bar twice. Now the document contains only body text.

3. Open the Reveal Codes area, where you can see the codes that control the outline, and then press Ctrl+Home,Ctrl+Home to

move the insertion point to the beginning of the outline (before the Outline code).

Removing codes with Find And Replace

4. The easiest way to remove the Outline codes from the beginning and end of the document is with the Find And Replace command. Choose Find And Replace from the Edit menu, and in the Find And Replace Text dialog box, choose Codes from the dialog box's Match menu to display this dialog box:

5. Select Outline in the Find Codes list box, click the Insert button to insert that code in the Find edit box, and then click Replace All in the Find And Replace Text dialog box to replace all Outline codes with nothing.

6. Click Close to close the Find And Replace Text dialog box. In the Reveal Codes area, the Outline codes are now gone.

7. Close the Reveal Codes area, and click the Close button on the Outline Bar to remove the bar from your screen.

8. Save REPORT.WPD, which is now a regular document.

Introducing Styles

WordPerfect includes a Styles feature that you can use to add formatting to specific document elements, such as headings. By assigning styles to these elements, you can maintain consistency throughout your documents. For example, if all first level headings are assigned the *Heading 1* style and you decide to change the formatting for first level headings, you can simply change the *Heading 1* style, and WordPerfect sees to it that all the first level headings are changed accordingly. Because you can make sweeping changes with only a few mouse clicks, you'll find that styles are real time-savers.

WordPerfect's styles

WordPerfect ships with several predefined styles, called *system styles*, for various elements of a document, including headings, outlines, headers and footers, and footnotes. When you create one of these elements, WordPerfect automatically displays the element in the appropriate system style unless you apply a different one. If you edit the system style, you can restore it to its default definition by selecting Reset from the Options drop-down list in the Style List dialog box.

Let's assign one of WordPerfect's predefined styles to the title in REPORT.WPD:

1. Move the insertion point to the end of the report's title, and press Enter twice to add some space below the title.

2. Display the Format Toolbar by right-clicking the current Toolbar and choosing Format from the QuickMenu. As you'll see, the Format Toolbar puts many of the features we'll use to format the report at our fingertips.

The Format Toolbar

3. Move the insertion point back to the report's title, and click the Styles button on the Toolbar (you may have to scroll the Toolbar) to display this dialog box:

The Styles button

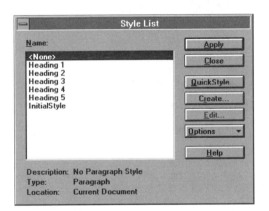

4. Click the *Heading 1* style in the Name list box, and click the Apply button to close the dialog box and apply the selected style to the report's title, as shown here:

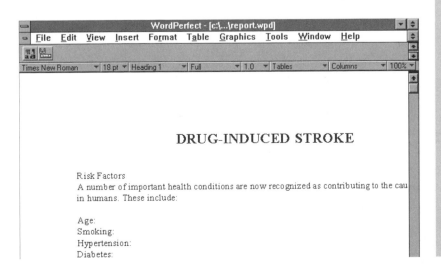

QuickStyle

To quickly create a style, click an insertion point in a paragraph that contains the formatting you want to use as the basis for your style. Next choose Styles from the Format menu to display the Style List dialog box. Click the QuickStyle button, enter a name and a description for the style, specify the style type, and then click OK and then Close to return to the document window. You can then apply the QuickStyle to text just as you would apply any other style.

Notice that Heading 1 now appears in the Select Style box on the Power Bar and at the left end of the status bar.

Let's create a new style for the report's second level headings:

1. Move the insertion point to the *Risk Factors* heading, and click the Styles button on the Toolbar.

2. In the Style List dialog box, click the Create button to display this Styles Editor dialog box:

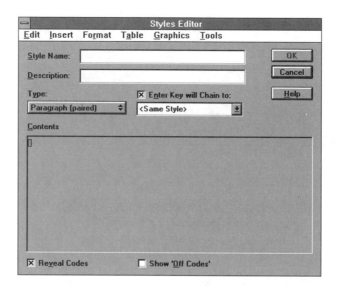

3. Type *Head 2* in the Style Name edit box. (We use the name *Head 2* because *Heading 2* is already assigned to one of WordPerfect's predefined styles.)

4. Type *Second Level Headings* in the Description edit box, and then click the Contents box.

To format the *Head 2* style, you make selections directly from the Styles Editor's menu bar. Try the following:

1. Choose Font from the Format menu to display the Font dialog box, and click the Bold option to add bold to the *Head 2* style.

2. Next point to the Relative Size option, hold down the mouse button, and select Large from the pop-up list to add the large size to the *Head 2* style.

3. Click OK to return to the Styles Editor dialog box.

Editing styles

You can edit WordPerfect's system styles or your own styles by selecting the style's name in the Style List dialog box and clicking the Edit button. WordPerfect displays the Styles Editor with the codes for the selected style in the Contents box. You can then modify the codes, clicking OK when you have adjusted the style to your satisfaction.

Now before you go any further, you need to define a stopping point for the *Head 2* style; otherwise, when you apply the *Head 2* style, all subsequent text will also be defined with that style. Follow these steps:

1. Click the down arrow below the Enter Key Will Chain To option, and select *<None>* from the drop-down list. Now when you press the Enter key to start a new paragraph, the style will automatically be turned off.

Turning off a style

2. Click OK to return to the Style List dialog box, and then double-click the *Head 2* style to close the Style List dialog box and apply the newly created style to *Risk Factors*.

3. Move the insertion point to the end of the heading, and press Enter to further set off the heading.

Whenever you create a style in WordPerfect, it is automatically added to the Select Style drop-down list on the Power Bar so that it is within easy reach. Apply the *Head 2* style to the *Drugs* heading by following these steps:

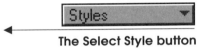

The Select Style button

1. Move the insertion point to *Drugs*, and click the Select Style button on the Power Bar to display the list of styles.

2. Click the *Head 2* style. Then add a blank line below the heading to set it off, and save the report.

The style you just created is a paragraph style. As you've seen, when you apply this type of style to a paragraph, the entire paragraph is affected. WordPerfect also offers character styles, which you can apply to a text selection rather than an entire paragraph. Character styles can save you time by allowing you to apply a number of attributes to a text selection in just a couple of steps. For the report's third level headings, let's create a character style that incorporates a different font and bold and italic:

1. Move the insertion point to the *Age* heading, and click the Styles button on the Toolbar.

2. In the Style List dialog box, click the Create button to open the Styles Editor dialog box.

3. Type *Head 3* in the Style Name edit box, type *Third Level Headings* in the Description edit box, and then click the Contents box.

4. Choose Font from the Styles Editor's Format menu, and when the Font dialog box appears, select a different font (we selected Arial), click the Bold and Italic options, and then click OK.

5. Click the Type option, select Character (paired) from the pop-up list, and then click OK.

6. Click Close in the Style List dialog box to return to the document window.

Now apply the new style by following these steps:

1. Select the *Age* heading, including the colon.

2. Click the Select Style button on the Power Bar, and then click the Head 3 style.

3. Repeat steps 1 and 2 for the six remaining level three headings, and then save the report.

The style you just created is available only for this document. You can save the current style list in a separate file so that if you want to use its styles in other WordPerfect documents all you have to do is retrieve the "style file." Here's how to save the list:

1. Click the Styles button on the Toolbar. In the Style List dialog box, click the Options button, and choose Save As to display this dialog box:

Chaining styles

The Enter Key Will Chain To option in the Styles Editor dialog box lets you set up a series of "chained" styles so that each time you press Enter, Word-Perfect automatically applies the next style in the chain. For example, suppose the ordinary paragraph style for a report has a 1/2-inch first-line indent but you want the first paragraph following a heading to have no first-line indent. You can specify that the style for headings should chain to the style for the no-indent paragraph. The no-indent paragraph style should then chain to the style for ordinary first-line indent paragraphs, which should in turn chain to another first-line indent paragraph by means of the <Same Style> setting. With these styles established, pressing Enter after typing a heading automatically starts a paragraph with no indent, and pressing Enter after that paragraph automatically starts the next and subsequent paragraphs with first-line indents.

2. Type *report.sty* in the Filename edit box, and press Enter to save the style list as a file. Click Close to return to the document window.

Now if you want to use the REPORT.STY style list for any other WordPerfect document, all you have to do is click Options in the Style List dialog box, choose Retrieve, and enter *report.sty* in the Filename edit box of the Retrieve Styles From dialog box.

Using style files

Our discussion of styles has been necessarily brief; however, you are now armed with enough information to explore this topic further on your own.

Storing and Retrieving Often-Used Text

To help you enter often-used text efficiently, accurately, and consistently, WordPerfect has two special features: Abbreviations and QuickCorrect. At first glance these two features seem almost identical; they both enable you to store text with a name and then insert the text in any document at any time simply by typing the name. And, unlike the contents of the Clipboard, Abbreviations and QuickCorrect entries are saved from one WordPerfect session to the next. So what's the difference between them? To insert an abbreviation, you type the abbreviation's name and then press Ctrl+A. To insert a QuickCorrect entry, you simply type the name; the instant you press the Spacebar to move on to the next word, WordPerfect automatically replaces the name with its entry.

Tables of contents, lists, indexes, cross-references, and tables of authorities

To create a table of contents for your document, start by marking the entries. Choose Table Of Contents from the Tools menu (or display the Generate Toolbar, and click the Table of Contents button), and select the text you want to include in the table of contents (for example, a heading in a report). On the Table Of Contents Feature Bar, click the Mark button corresponding to the level (from 1 through 5) that you want to assign to the entry. Repeat these steps until all the entries are marked. Then position the insertion point where you want the table of contents to appear (remember to allow enough space for all the marked entries, perhaps including a page break to separate the table of contents from your document), and click the Define button on the Table Of Contents Feature Bar. In the Define Table Of Contents dialog box, specify the number of levels (1 through 5) and their page number positions, and click OK. (You can also change the table of content's style, numbering scheme, and so on in this dialog box.) Finally, click the Generate button on the Table Of Contents Feature Bar, and click OK. Using the List, Index, Cross-Reference, and Table Of Authorities commands on the Tools menu, you can follow this same general procedure to create lists (figures, tables, and so on), indexes, cross-references, and tables of authorities for your documents.

How do you decide which to use? Here's an example. Suppose you own a landscaping business. You know you'd save a lot of time and effort if you could type *aspen* instead of having to type and italicize *Populus tremuloides* (the botanical name for the aspen tree) every time you include this tree in a materials list for your wholesaler. But when you communicate with your clients, you want to be able to refer to the aspen tree by its common name rather than its botanical name. This entry is a prime candidate for Abbreviations because you can control when WordPerfect replaces the name *aspen* with the entry *Populus tremuloides* and when it stays plain old *aspen*. If you use QuickCorrect instead, WordPerfect will always replace the name *aspen* with *Populus tremuloides*. Let's try both features.

Using Abbreviations

As we said, you use WordPerfect's Abbreviations feature to store text that you want to be able to retrieve manually. For this example, we'll turn an existing word into an abbreviation. Follow along as we simplify the typing of *stroke*:

1. Position the insertion point after the colon at the end of the *Age* heading.

2. Type a space, and then type

   The incidence of stroke

Creating abbreviations → 3. Double-click the word *stroke* to select it, and choose Abbreviations from the Insert menu to display this dialog box:

4. Click the Create button to display this Create Abbreviation dialog box:

5. Type *s* in the Abbreviation Name edit box, and click OK to close the Create Abbreviation dialog box. Then click Close to close the Abbreviations dialog box.

Follow these steps to use the abbreviation:

1. Type a space after the word *stroke*, and continue the paragraph as follows:

increases dramatically with age. The chances of s

2. With the insertion point immediately to the right of the *s*, press Ctrl+A (for *Abbreviation*) to expand the abbreviation *s* into the full word *stroke*.

3. Now continue the paragraph, pressing Ctrl+A after *s* to insert the word *stroke* where indicated.

are very small in young individuals. A sharp increase in the risk of stroke *occurs in the population beyond 50 years of age.*

4. Press Enter once to add some space. This is the result:

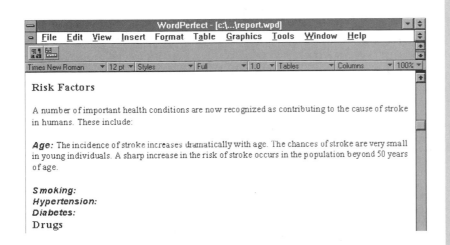

Using abbreviations

Using abbreviations in other documents

When you create an abbreviation, it is associated with the template on which the current document is based. If you want to use the abbreviation with documents based on a different template, you can copy the abbreviation to that template by choosing Abbreviations from the Insert menu, clicking the Copy button in the Abbreviations dialog box, selecting the template containing the abbreviation, selecting the abbreviation itself, and then selecting the template to which you want to copy the abbreviation.

Now all you have to do to insert the word *stroke* anywhere in the report is to repeat step 2 above. This may seem like a trivial example, but imagine the impact on your efficiency if the report included 20 instances of *acetylcholinesterase* or *Rebecca Brand v. Midvalley Clinic*, instead of *stroke*.

5. Enter the following paragraph after the *Smoking* heading to get an idea of the time you can save with abbreviations:

   Smoking is a well-established risk for stroke. *The longer an individual has smoked and the more they have smoked, the higher the risk of* stroke *as well as heart attack. It is now known that cessation of smoking at any time, despite the duration of smoking, will significantly reduce the risk of coronary disease and heart attack. Whether the same is true for* stroke *has yet to be demonstrated, but in all likelihood the same will apply.*

6. Press Enter to add a blank line below the paragraph, and then save the document.

Using QuickCorrect

Because WordPerfect automatically replaces QuickCorrect names with their entries, you should assign unique sequences of characters that you are not likely to use normally in a document as the names of QuickCorrect entries. Try this:

1. Click an insertion point after the *Hypertension* heading, type a space, and then type this:

   The risk of stroke *increases, as does that of heart disease, in humans who have elevated blood pressure.*

2. Select *blood pressure*, and choose QuickCorrect from the Tools menu to display this dialog box:

Bypassing QuickCorrect

To turn off QuickCorrect, deselect the Replace Text As You Type option in the QuickCorrect dialog box. If you don't want to turn off QuickCorrect but you also don't want QuickCorrect to replace a particular instance of a name with its entry, type the name, and after QuickCorrect replaces it, click the Undo button (see page 32).

As you can see, WordPerfect is waiting for you to enter the name that you want replaced with the selected text, which appears in the With edit box. Taking up the majority of the QuickCorrect dialog box is a ready-made list of "words" to be replaced each time you type them.

3. In the Replace edit box, type *bp* as the name of the entry, and click Add Entry. WordPerfect adds the name and its replacement to the list.

4. Click Close to return to the document window.

Now let's use this QuickCorrect entry so that you can get a feel for what a time-saver it can be:

1. Click an insertion point after *blood pressure*, type a period and a space, and then type this:

    It has now been demonstrated by clinical trials that control of bp *is a major factor in reducing the incidence of* stroke. *Furthermore, the sooner increased* bp *is diagnosed and treated, the greater the reduction of* stroke *as well as heart attack.*

2. Press Enter to add a blank line below the paragraph.

3. Next, click an insertion point after the *Diabetes* heading, type a space, and then type the following:

    Diabetes and some other chronic illnesses are associated with an increase in the incidence of stroke. *Diabetics who do not smoke or have high* bp *are less likely to suffer stroke. Whether strict control of diabetes itself (maintaining as*

QuickCorrect options

If you click the Options button in the QuickCorrect dialog box, you are presented with several options that take care of common typing "errors." By default, WordPerfect corrects faulty capitalization—sentences that don't begin with a capital letter and two initial capital letters in a word— and changes double spaces within a sentence to a single space. (You can also opt to change a single space at the end of a sentence to a double space and vice versa.) In addition, WordPerfect changes both single and double straight-quotation marks to open and close ("smart") quotation marks. You can turn off any of these options by clicking the corresponding check box.

normal a blood sugar level as possible) reduces the risk of
stroke *is unknown at this time, but long-range clinical studies*
are in progress.

4. Press Enter to add a blank line below the paragraph, and then
save the document.

Creating Numbered Lists

If you look at the printouts on page 89, you'll see that the
sample report contains a numbered list under the heading
Drugs That Damage Blood Vessels. Generally, you use numbered lists for step-by-step instructions or sequential processes. WordPerfect has a Bullets & Numbers feature that
makes short work of creating lists, and we'll use this feature
to create a bulleted list in the next section. However, we'll use
a different technique for the numbered list so that we can show
you how to indent paragraphs from both the left and right
margins and how to set custom tabs to align items exactly as
you want them. Start by typing the paragraph that precedes
the numbered list:

1. Click an insertion point after the colon in the *Drugs That*
Damage Blood Vessels heading, type a space, and then type
the following paragraph. (Remember to type an *s* and press
Ctrl+A to insert the word *stroke*.)

A few drugs used for long periods of time can damage blood
vessels, which weakens their walls and, in the case of arteries
in the brain, may lead to stroke. *How these drugs produce*
this effect is not clear, but it is thought that it occurs in the
following steps:

2. Press Enter twice to add a blank line.

The Double Indent button

3. Press the Tab key once, type *1.* (be sure to include the period),
and click the Double Indent button on the Toolbar. Then type

With continual administration over long periods of time, the
drug accumulates in the cells that line the artery.

and press Enter twice to start the second numbered item.

4. Press Tab, type *2.*, click the Double Indent button, and type

As the drug accumulates, it gradually inhibits the cells'
metabolic processes.

and then press Enter twice. Don't be alarmed if WordPerfect inserts a soft page break at this point; the position of the page break will change as you edit the text.

Soft page breaks

5. Press Tab, type *3.*, click the Double Indent button, and type

Eventually the cells of the artery die, leaving the vessel wall
weakened and vulnerable.

Press Enter just once this time. Here's the result:

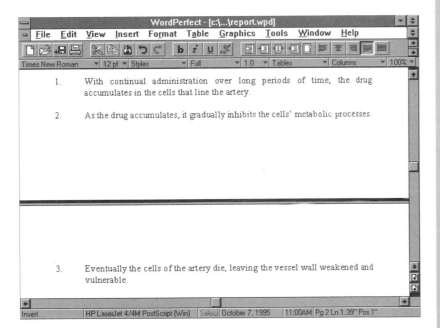

So far, so good. But using the default tab settings produced a rather large space between the numbers and their corresponding text. Let's tighten up this space a bit by setting a custom tab at the beginning of the list. Follow the steps on the next page to make this adjustment.

Make it fit!

If you've ever written 30 pages of material for a 25-page term paper (or vice versa), you'll appreciate WordPerfect's Make It Fit Expert. By adjusting elements such as margins, font size, and line spacing, the Make It Fit Expert can shrink or expand a document to fill a specified number of pages. Simply click the Make It Fit button on the Toolbar. When the Expert's dialog box appears, specify the number of pages you want the document to fill (the current page count is listed at the top of the dialog box), specify the elements the Expert can adjust, and then click the Make It Fit button. A message appears, displaying the number of passes the Expert is taking to make the document fit. When the Expert is finished, you return to the document window. If you're not satisfied with the result, you can click the Undo button on the Toolbar to return the document to its original state.

The Tab Set button

1. Place the insertion point just before the 1 in the first numbered list item, and click the Tab Set button on the Toolbar to display this dialog box:

The Ruler Bar now appears below the Power Bar so that you can see the exact location of the tabs you set.

2. In the Settings group box, leave the Type option set to Left, change the Position setting to *0.75*, and click Set to set a left-aligned tab three-quarters of an inch from the left margin. (Notice that the Left Margin (Relative) option is selected in the Position From group box.) Click OK to return to the document window. The result is shown on the facing page.

WordPerfect macros

If you find that you often repeat a series of commands, you might be able to use a macro—a specialized mini-program—to have WordPerfect automate that task for you. WordPerfect provides several prerecorded macros. To run one of these macros, choose Macro and then Play from the Tools menu. The Play Macro dialog box appears, displaying a list of available macros. At the bottom of this dialog box, WordPerfect displays a description of the macro highlighted in the list. Select the macro you want to use, and then click Play to run the macro. You can also record commands and save them as a macro. To create a macro, simply choose Macro and then Record from the Tools menu. Then enter a name for the macro in the Record Macro dialog box (WordPerfect supplies the WCM extension), and click Record. The Macro Edit Feature Bar appears, *MacroRecord* is displayed in dimmed letters in the status bar, and the pointer changes to a circle with a slash through it when it is over the text of the document. Now perform the steps necessary to carry out the desired action. When you finish, click the Stop button on the Macro Edit Bar or choose Macro and Record from the Tools menu. To play back the macro, choose Macro and then Play from the Tools menu, select the macro's name, and click Play. If you want to assign a macro to the current template, choose Template Macro from the Tools menu, and then follow the procedure described above. (Template macros are only available when the template to which they are assigned is in use.)

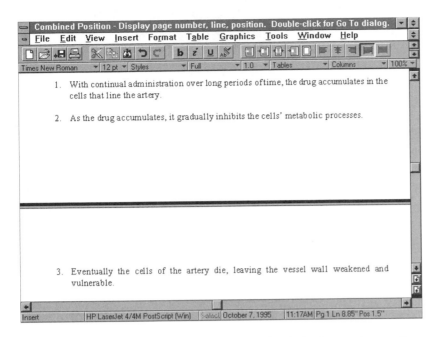

Now you must return the tabs to their default settings after the numbered list so that the tab setting at 0.75 inch doesn't affect the rest of the report. This time, we'll use the Ruler Bar:

1. Move the insertion point to the beginning of the *Qnifen and Fiszol* heading, and choose Ruler Bar from the View menu to display the Ruler Bar like this:

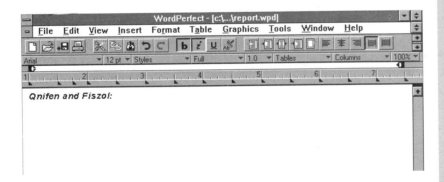

2. On the Ruler Bar, point to the triangle designating the tab at the 1.75-inch mark (the Ruler Bar measures from the edge of the page and reflects the 1-inch left margin), hold down the mouse button, drag the tab away from the ruler, and release

Tab leaders

The four types of tabs—Left, Center, Right, and Decimal—are all blank, meaning that the space they control contains no characters. You can set these four types of tabs with leaders so that Word-Perfect fills the space they control with a specified character. The default leader character is a dot, but in the Tab Set dialog box, you can replace the dot in the Dot Leader Character edit box with any character you choose. For example, you might want to use the underscore as the leader character for fill-in lines in forms. You can also change the space between leader characters by adjusting the Spaces Between Characters setting.

the mouse button. The tab disappears, indicating that only the default half-inch tabs are in effect from the insertion point on.

3. Choose Ruler Bar from the View menu to turn off the Ruler Bar, and then save the report.

Creating Bulleted Lists

If you look back at the report shown at the beginning of the chapter, you'll see a bulleted list near the bottom of the first page. Generally, you use bullets for lists of items that are not sequential or hierarchical. For this example, we'll use Word-Perfect's Bullets & Numbers feature, which really simplifies the process. Start by typing the paragraph that precedes the list:

1. Click an insertion point after the colon in the *Drugs That Stimulate Blood Pressure* heading, type a space, and then type the following. (Use the *bp* QuickCorrect entry where indicated.)

   This first class of drugs includes adrenalin, amphetamines, and cocaine. Adrenalin is used therapeutically to raise bp, *whereas amphetamines and cocaine are commonly abused for their stimulatory effects. The principal actions of all these drugs are:*

2. Press Enter twice, and then type the following lines, pressing Enter once after each one:

   Increase bp
   Increase heart rate
   Stimulate brain

3. To turn these three lines into a bulleted list, select all three, and choose Bullets & Numbers from the Insert menu to display this dialog box:

Using other bullet characters

WordPerfect's five bullet styles should meet most needs, but it's easy enough to create custom bullets for those occasions when you want something special. After choosing Bullets & Numbers from the Insert menu, select a style that you use infrequently, and then click the Edit button. In the Styles Editor dialog box, delete the bullet character, and then choose Character from the Insert menu to display the WordPerfect Characters dialog box. Select a character set from the Character Set drop-down list, and then select the character you want from the Characters box. (For example, you can give your bullets more weight by selecting a character such as the pointing hand, ☞, in the Iconic Symbols character set.) Click Insert And Close to return to the Styles Editor, where the code for the character has been inserted in the Contents box, and then complete the editing process as usual.

4. As you can see, you have a choice of several bullet styles. For this example, click Square in the Styles list box, and then click OK. Here's the result:

Pretty slick! But suppose you want the bulleted list to look more like the numbered list we created earlier. You could manually adjust each item in the list, but here's a quicker way:

1. With the insertion point located in any of the bulleted items, click the Styles button on the Toolbar. WordPerfect displays the Style List dialog box, which now includes a style for square bullets.

2. The square bullet style is selected, so click Edit in the Style List dialog box to display the Styles Editor dialog box shown on the next page.

Other Ruler Bar actions

Above the rule on the Ruler Bar are markers that indicate the positions of the left and right margins and the indents in effect for the current paragraph. You can adjust these elements of the paragraph by dragging the appropriate marker to the left or right. Grabbing hold of the correct marker takes a sure hand, but with a little practice, you'll find that manipulating the margins and indents of your documents with the Ruler Bar is often quicker than working through the equivalent dialog boxes.

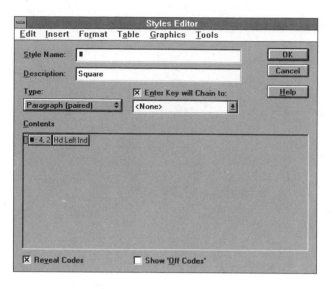

3. Choose Tab from the bottom of the Styles Editor's Insert menu to insert a Left Tab code in front of the bullet in the Contents box.

4. Click OK to close the Styles Editor dialog box, and then click Close to close the Style List dialog box. In the document window, WordPerfect has adjusted the three bulleted items to reflect the edited style.

5. Now choose Ruler Bar from the View menu, select the three bulleted items, point to the 1.75-inch mark on the Ruler Bar, and click to set a custom left-aligned tab like the one used for the numbered list. Then turn off the Ruler Bar, and save the report. Here are the results:

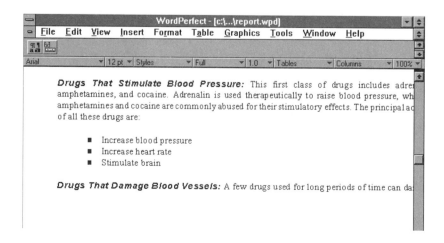

Because you selected the three items before setting the tab, WordPerfect has entered beginning and ending tab codes around the selection, so this time you don't have to worry about resetting the tabs for the rest of the document.

Creating Parallel Columns

In this section, we'll explore ways to use WordPerfect's Columns feature to format information so that it is readily accessible to your report's readers. Here, we'll take a look at parallel columns, which allow you to present unequal columns of information side-by-side. WordPerfect also enables you to create newspaper-style columns, which "snake" from top to bottom and from left to right across the page (see the adjacent tip).

Parallel columns, also called *side-by-side paragraphs*, are useful for creating documents such as inventory descriptions and presentation notes. The easiest way to understand this concept is to look at an example. In the report shown at the beginning of the chapter, parallel columns are used in the middle of the second page to summarize the drugs Qnifen and Fiszol. You cannot use tabs or indents to create parallel columns; you must use WordPerfect's Columns feature.

Start by following these steps to write a lead-in paragraph for the parallel-column format:

1. Click an insertion point after the colon in the *Qnifen and Fiszol* heading, type a space, and then type the following, using the stroke abbreviation:

   Both of these drugs are used to treat osteoporosis (softening of the bone). Both have also been associated with stroke, *but to varying degrees. A summary description of the drugs is given below:*

2. Press Enter twice to insert a blank line and start a new one.

   Now set up the parallel columns by following the steps on the next page.

Newspaper columns

To create ordinary newspaper columns in WordPerfect (where the text "snakes" from one column to the next), simply select the number of columns (from 2 to 5) from the Columns Define dropdown list on the Power Bar. To create newspaper columns that will be adjusted so that they are equal in length, display the Columns dialog box, and select the Balanced Newspaper option. You can even insert graphics in your columns to give them that extra-professional look (see Chapter 6 for more information about graphics).

The Columns Define button

1. Click the Columns Define button on the Power Bar to display a drop-down list of options, and select Define to display the Columns dialog box:

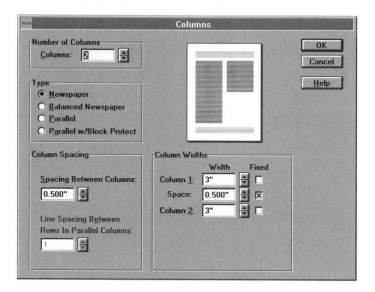

2. Select the Parallel option in the Type group box, accept the default settings for the other options, and click OK.

   Now you're ready to enter the column text:

1. Type

   Qnifen was the first drug developed for the treatment of osteoporosis. However, after several years of use, it became associated with stroke.

2. Select Column Break from the Columns Define drop-down list on the Power Bar (or press Ctrl+Enter) to move the insertion point to the top of the second column, and type this:

   Fiszol was recently approved for the treatment of osteoporosis. Because Fiszol has a different structure than Qnifen, current theory is that Fiszol will not have the same side effects. However, clinical trials have not yet corroborated this theory.

3. Select Column Break from the Columns Define drop-down list. The parallel columns look like this:

Instant columns

To turn existing normal text into column text, select the text, select the Define option from the Columns Define drop-down list on the Power Bar, and specify how you want the columns to appear in the Columns dialog box. Then, to break the text into actual columns, position the insertion point where you want the break to occur, and select Column Break from the Columns Define drop-down list (or press Ctrl+Enter).

4. Turn off parallel columns by selecting Columns Off from the Columns Define drop-down list.

5. Save the report by clicking the Save button.

Navigating from column to column is very easy. You can move to the top or bottom of the current column by pressing Alt+Home or Alt+End, and you can move one column to the left or right by pressing Alt+Left Arrow or Alt+Right Arrow. You can edit and format the text in columns just like normal text, including changing margins, justification, and so on. In addition, you can use the options in the Columns dialog box to change the number of columns (you can have up to 24), the space between columns, the line spacing between rows, and the width of columns. You can also add borders and shading to columns by choosing Columns and then Border/Fill from the Format menu and specifying options in the Column Border dialog box the same way you would specify them in the Paragraph Border dialog box (see page 62).

← Navigating in columns

Adding Footnotes

Some reports are more likely to have footnotes than others. If you use information from outside sources or want to steer readers toward data that backs up your arguments, you'll probably want to give credit or bibliographic information in footnotes, rather than cluttering up the body of the report.

In this section, we show you how to create the footnote located on page 2 of the sample report at the beginning of the chapter. This footnote occurs in a paragraph that follows the parallel columns, so start by typing the text of the paragraph:

1. Press Ctrl+End to position the insertion point at the end of the report, and type the following, using the stroke abbreviation where appropriate:

   Although both Qnifen and Fiszol appear to be equally effective in treating osteoporosis, they differ greatly in their chemical structures. While Qnifen contains one methyl group (CH3), Fiszol has none. This structural difference may explain why patients taking Qnifen have a higher incidence of stroke *than patients taking Fiszol. The following statement was recently published in the New World Journal of Medicine:*

2. Press Enter twice to start a new paragraph. (If you want, italicize the journal name and then subscript the 3 in *CH3* by selecting the 3, choosing Font from the Format menu, and changing the Position option to Subscript.)

3. With the insertion point located at the end of the report, click the Double Indent button on the Toolbar to indent the next paragraph—a quotation—from both the left and right margins. Now type the following:

   Early reports of fewer cases of stroke *associated with Fiszol would indicate that at this time, Fiszol is a better choice than Qnifen in the treatment of osteoporosis.*

4. Save the report by clicking the Save button.

   Now we'll create the footnote:

1. With the insertion point positioned just after the period in the quotation, choose Footnote and then Create from the Insert menu. (To create endnotes, which appear at the end of a document instead of at the bottom of their respective pages, you would choose Endnote instead.) WordPerfect inserts the footnote reference number 1 at the end of the quotation, draws a line across the bottom of the window, and enters the number of the footnote, ready for you to type its text. It also displays

Adding comments

To add a comment to a WordPerfect document, choose Comment and then Create from the Insert menu. WordPerfect displays the Comment Feature Bar and a window in which you type your comment. You can click buttons to add your name, the date, or the time to the comment, and click the Close button to return to the document. The comment itself is hidden; however, WordPerfect displays a bubble containing quotation marks in the margin adjacent to the line containing the comment. To see the comment, simply click the bubble. Click it again to hide the comment. Comments don't affect your document text when it's printed. (To print your comments as part of the document, choose Comment and then Convert To Text from the Insert menu.)

the Footnote Feature Bar, which contains buttons that are useful for working with footnotes.

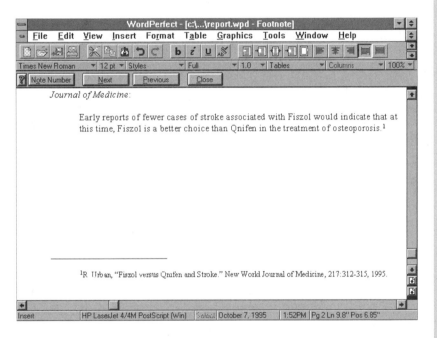

← **The Footnote Feature Bar**

2. Type the text of the footnote:

   R. Urban, "Fiszol versus Qnifen and Stroke." New World Journal of Medicine, 217:312-315, 1995.

3. Next select the entire footnote, choose Font from the Format menu, select Small as the Relative Size option, and click OK. Here are the results:

4. Click the Close button on the Footnote Bar to remove the bar from the screen.

   You can use this procedure to add footnotes anywhere in your document. For each footnote, WordPerfect inserts a Footnote code. If you insert a new footnote before an existing footnote, WordPerfect renumbers the existing footnote. For example, if you add a footnote to page 1 of the report, WordPerfect changes the number of the footnote you just created to 2. You can delete a footnote by deleting the Footnote code in the Reveal Codes area or by deleting the footnote reference number in the document window. When you delete a footnote, WordPerfect automatically renumbers any remaining footnotes in the document.

Footnote options

You can change the footnote numbers, edit the Footnote style, and access a whole host of other options by choosing Footnote and then Options from the Insert menu. For example, to change the default Arabic numbers to lowercase Roman numbers, select the Lowercase Roman option from the Method pop-up list in the Footnote Options dialog box. To edit WordPerfect's default Footnote style, click the In Text or In Note button in the Edit Numbering Style group box, and make the necessary changes in the Styles Editor dialog box. What about changing the footnote separator line? Simply click the Separator button, and make your changes in the Line Separator dialog box. You can change the line's spacing, position, length, and style; and if you prefer no line at all, just select <None> as the Line Style option. The options in the Footnote Options dialog box also allow you to specify the amount of spacing between consecutive footnotes and whether or not to include a *(continued...)* message for footnotes that are continued on another page.

When you add a footnote to a document, WordPerfect places the footnote at the bottom of the page on which the reference number occurs and separates the footnote from the main text with a 2-inch line. If the footnote is too long to fit entirely on the page, at least the amount of footnote text specified in the Amount Of Footnote To Keep Together option is retained on the same page as its reference number (see the tip on page 117). If the footnote won't fit, WordPerfect breaks the page, moving both the text containing the reference number and the footnote to the next page.

Adding Page Headers

Take a look at page 2 of the report shown at the beginning of the chapter. This page has a *header* at the top. A header is a line of text containing information, such as a report title, a date, or the name of your company, that you want to appear on the pages of your document. The advantage of using a header is that you create it once and then leave it up to WordPerfect to place it at the top of the pages for you. You can have two different headers on a page, and you can specify on which pages they should appear.

Here's how to create a header for page 2 of the report:

1. Be sure the insertion point is located on the second page. (For the headers to work properly, the insertion point must be located on the page where you want the header to first appear.)

2. Choose Header/Footer from the Format menu to display this dialog box:

3. With the Header A option selected, click the Create button. WordPerfect closes the dialog box and moves the insertion point to the top of the second page so that you can enter the

Bookmarks and Quick-Marks

Use bookmarks and QuickMarks to mark specific places in a document so that you can quickly return to those places during subsequent work sessions. A QuickMark is a generic bookmark that you can go to by simply pressing Ctrl+Q. You can have only one QuickMark in each document. Bookmarks are more work to get to, but you can have several of them in a document. To create a QuickMark, choose Bookmark from the Insert menu, and in the Bookmark dialog box, click the Set Quick-Mark button. Later, jump to the QuickMark by pressing Ctrl+Q. When you set a QuickMark, the existing QuickMark is removed. To create a more stable marker, use a bookmark instead. Choose Bookmark from the Insert menu, click the Create button, assign a name to the bookmark, and then click OK. The Bookmark dialog box lists all the bookmarks you have created. You can select one, and click Go To to move to its location.

text of the header. It also displays the Header/Footer Feature Bar, which contains buttons that are useful for working with headers and footers.

The Header/Footer
Feature Bar

4. Type *Fox & Associates*. Then choose Line and Flush Right from the Format menu, and type *Drug-Induced Stroke*. The header looks like this:

5. Click Close on the Header/Footer Bar to remove the bar from the screen.

6. If you're interested, display the Reveal Codes area, and check out the Header code that WordPerfect inserted at the beginning of the paragraph where the insertion point was located when you chose Header/Footer. Then save the report.

You can change a header by clicking Edit in the Headers/ Footers dialog box and then editing the header just as you would edit text in the document window. For practice, let's format the new header:

1. Choose Header/Footer from the Format menu, and with Header A selected, click the Edit button. The insertion point moves to the beginning of the header.

2. To make the header italic and small, select the entire header, and choose the Font command from the Format menu. In the Font dialog box, click the Italic check box, change the Relative Size option to Small, and then click OK.

Delaying codes

The Delay Codes feature lets you tell WordPerfect on which pages you want elements such as headers, footers, and page numbers to be printed. For example, you might want to delay printing headers and page numbers on pages that are occupied by large graphics or tables. To use Delay Codes, choose Page and then Delay Codes from the Format menu, and enter the number of pages you want to skip before the codes go into effect. When you click OK, WordPerfect displays the Define Delayed Codes window, in which you enter the codes using menu commands or the buttons on the Delay Codes Feature Bar. Click Close to return to the document window with the codes delayed for the specified number of pages. (Note that you can delay any open code, such as Justification, Margins, and Page Numbering; but you can't delay paired codes, such as Bold and Italics.)

3. Click the Close button to remove the Header/Footer Bar, and then click the Save button to save the report before moving on to the next section.

Numbering Pages

WordPerfect's Page Numbering feature is easy to use and efficient. You can print numbers in one of eight different positions on the page and in one of five different numbering schemes—Arabic (1, 2, 3), lowercase letters (a, b, c), upper-case letters (A, B, C), lowercase Roman (i, ii, iii), or uppercase Roman (I, II, III). Follow these steps to number the pages of the report:

1. Move the insertion point to the first page of the report (where you want page numbering to begin).

2. Choose Page and Numbering from the Format menu to display the Page Numbering dialog box:

Line numbering

Line numbers are useful in documents such as legal contracts, where specific lines might need to be referenced. To turn on line numbering, choose Line and then Numbering from the Format menu, and in the Line Numbering dialog box, click the Turn Line Numbering On check box to select it. Then select a Numbering Method option, and specify the starting number and the interval between numbers (for example, you might display a number for every fifth line). You can specify the number position, whether numbers should start at 1 on each page, and whether blank lines and newspaper columns should be counted.

3. Point to the Position option, hold down the mouse button, and select Bottom Center from the pop-up list to print a page number at the bottom center of every page.

4. Next click the Options button to display the Page Numbering Options dialog box, click an insertion point in front of [Pg #] in the Format And Accompanying Text edit box, and type *Page* and a space. The dialog box now looks like this:

Notice that the sample boxes show *Page 2* and *Page 3*.

5. Click OK to return to the Page Numbering dialog box, and then click the Font button to display the Page Numbering Font dialog box. Change the Size option to Small, and click OK.

Changing the size of page numbers

6. Click OK to return to the document, and then save the report.

Turning on page numbers inserts page numbering codes in your document. You can see the codes at the beginning of the report in the Reveal Codes area, and you can check out the numbers themselves by scrolling to the bottom of each page.

Customizing page numbers

In the Page Numbering Options dialog box, you can add secondary page numbers, chapter numbers, and volume numbers to your primary page numbers. (Secondary page numbers are useful if you've made major revisions to a document and you want to keep track of the "old" page numbers. Both the primary and secondary page numbers are incremented automatically.) For example, to number the pages of a multipart report in the format *Part A, Page 1*, you click an insertion point in front of [Pg #] in the Format And Accompanying Text edit box, type *Part* and a space, select Chapter Number from the Insert drop-down list to insert the [Chp #] code, and type a comma, a space, the word *Page*, and another space. Next you change the format of the Chapter option to Uppercase Letter. The sample boxes then show *Part A, Page 2* and *Part A, Page 3*. To number the pages of the next part in the format *Part B, Page 1*, you follow the same procedure, except that at the beginning of the document for Part B, you choose Page and then Numbering from the Format menu, click the Value button in the Page Numbering dialog box, and set the New Chapter Number option to 2 so that the [Chp #] code inserts B instead of A. You might want to experiment with the other options in the Numbering Value and Page Numbering Option dialog boxes to see their effects.

Visual Impact:
Adding Tables, Charts, and Graphics

*Import a graphic
and format it
as a logo*

The Fox Report

DRUG-INDUCED STROKE

Risk Factors

A number of important health
in humans. These include:

Age: The incidence of stroke
in young individuals. A sharp
of age.

Smoking: Smoking is a well
the more they have smoked, th
cessation of smoking at any ti
of coronary disease and heart
but in all likelihood the same

Hypertension: The risk of
elevated blood pressure. It has
is a major factor in reducing
pressure is diagnosed and tre

Diabetes: Diabetes and so
incidence of stroke. Diabetics
stroke. Whether strict contro
possible) reduces the risk of
progress.

Drugs

Three classes of drugs used th
with stroke.

Drugs That Stimulate
amphetamines, and cocaine.
amphetamines and cocaine are
of all these drugs are:

The following table compares the effects of adrenalin/cocaine, Qnifen, and Fiszol on such factors
as blood pressure, heart rate, and risk of stroke.

Percent Change			
Drug	Adrenalin/Cocaine	Qnifen	Fiszol
Blood Pressure	250.60	25.78	2.30
Heart Rate	5.78	2.70	-3.67
Brain Stimulation	12.00	-34.28	2.46
Bone Structure	0.00	520.80	489.20
Risk of Stroke	2.70	1.56	0.91

*Present your
data in an
easy-to-
understand
table*

PATIENT	GW	SH	BP	PJ	DE	CE	WD	TW	LD	GA	JK	AM
SEX	M	F	F	M	M	M	F	F	F	F	M	M
WEIGHT	178	124	132	198	205	212	156	127	117	167	179	158
BLOOD PRESSURE	152	120	145	134	168	136	127	140	128	137	148	143
PULSE	80	63	79	90	72	65	85	69	85	74	81	
EEG	4	8	9	8	7	5	3	7	8	5	4	
BONE DENSITY	23	16	12	31	30	24	17	14	20	10	22	32

*Import a
spreadsheet as
a WordPerfect
table*

The chart to the right is a graphic
representation of the data compiled in
the table above. This data was obtained
from a clinical study of 12 adult
patients who are currently undergoing
treatment for osteoporosis.

Clinical Profile

BONE DENSITY
EEG
PULSE
BLOOD PRESSURE
WEIGHT
SEX

*Use WordPerfect
to quickly chart
your table data*

Successful computer applications have to be versatile, and versatility is certainly WordPerfect's strong suit. In fact, strictly speaking, WordPerfect 6.1 for Windows is not just a word processor. You've always been able to use WordPerfect to create tables, but you can also include formulas and built-in spreadsheet functions in those tables, and you can generate charts based on the tables' data. On the graphics front, you can still import pictures created in other programs, and you can also use WordPerfect Draw to create your own images without ever having to leave WordPerfect. In this chapter, we briefly demonstrate how to dress up your documents with tables, charts, and graphics.

Setting Up Tables

Because tables are standard features of reports, presentations, and other business documents, WordPerfect goes to great lengths to make generating tables as painless as possible. You use the Tables feature to specify the number of columns and rows and then leave it to WordPerfect to put the whole thing together.

To demonstrate how easy the process is, we'll show you how to create the table shown at the beginning of the chapter. Start by typing a lead-in paragraph either at the end of the report created in Chapter 5 or in a new document:

1. If you are working in REPORT.WPD, press Ctrl+End to move to the end of the document, press Enter if necessary to add some space, and then press Ctrl+Enter to insert a page break so that the table will be on page 3 of the report.

2. Type the following, and then press Enter twice:

    The following table compares the effects of adrenalin/ cocaine, Qnifen, and Fiszol on such factors as blood pressure, heart rate, and risk of stroke.

3. Display the Tables Toolbar by right-clicking the Toolbar and choosing Tables from the QuickMenu.

Now you can start assembling the table:

The Table Expert

You can use WordPerfect's Table Expert to apply a table style to an existing table. Simply position the insertion point in the table, choose Expert from the Table menu (or click the Table Expert button on the Tables Toolbar), and select a style from the Available Styles list in the Table Expert dialog box (a sample of the selected style is displayed in the dialog box). When you're ready, click the Apply button. If you create a table style of your own, you can add that style to the Available Styles list by clicking the Create button in the Table Expert dialog box and naming the style. You can then use the Options button to delete or rename the style (you cannot delete or rename WordPerfect's predefined table styles). If you want new tables to be created with a particular style, simply select the style in the Table Expert dialog box, click the Initial Style button, and then click Yes.

The Table QuickCreate button

1. Point to the Table QuickCreate button on the Power Bar, and hold down the left mouse button to display a column/row grid.

2. Drag the mouse pointer across the first four columns and down the first six rows. When you release the mouse button, WordPerfect inserts this table structure in the document:

3. Choose Reveal Codes from the View menu and press the Down Arrow key to scroll through the table. The Tbl Def (for *table definition*) and Tbl Off codes tell WordPerfect where the table begins and ends. The Row and Cell codes tell WordPerfect where the rows and cells begin and end. Choose Reveal Codes again to close the Reveal Codes area.

A border surrounds the table, and borders also divide the columns and rows into cells. In the status bar, *TABLE A Cell A1* indicates that the insertion point is currently located in the cell at the intersection of the first column (column A) and the first row (row 1). Each cell in the table has a similar *address*, allowing you to quickly determine the position of the insertion point by watching the status bar. (If you click the Row/Column Indicators button on the Tables Toolbar, WordPerfect displays column letters and row numbers, which can also help orient you in the table.) Follow the steps on the next page to enter data in the table.

Floating cells

Suppose a mathematical formula in one of your tables calculates the total sales costs for your department, and you cite that total frequently in a report. If the total changes, you have to find and change each reference to the total throughout the report. To avoid mistakes, you can create the references as floating cells that refer to the cell in the table that contains the total. Then if the total changes, the values in the floating cells automatically change. When you have had some experience creating tables and using WordPerfect's spreadsheet functions, you might want to explore this feature further.

1. To enter the column headings, type *Percent Change* in cell A1, and then press the Tab key to move to cell B1. Type *Adrenalin/Cocaine*, and then press Tab to move to cell C1. Type *Fiszol*, and press Tab to move to cell D1. Finally, type *Qnifen*, and press Tab to move to cell A2.

Navigating in tables

2. Finish the table by typing the entries shown below, pressing Tab to move from cell to cell. (Pressing Shift+Tab moves the insertion point to the previous cell. You can also use the mouse and the Arrow keys to move around.)

Blood Pressure	*250.6*	*2.3*	*25.78*
Heart Rate	*5.78*	*-3.67*	*2.7*
Brain Stimulation	*12*	*2.46*	*-34.28*
Bone Structure	*0*	*489.2*	*520.8*
Risk of Stroke	*2.7*	*0.91*	*1.56*

3. Now save the document.

Rearranging Tables

You can easily rearrange the columns and rows in a table. Here's how to switch the Qnifen and Fiszol columns:

Selecting cells

1. Point to the top border of the cell containing the *Qnifen* heading, and when the pointer changes to a white arrow, click the mouse button to select the cell.

Moving Columns

2. Click the Cut button on the Toolbar. WordPerfect displays this dialog box:

3. Click the Column option, and then click OK. The *Qnifen* column disappears.

4. With the insertion point at the beginning of the *Fiszol* heading, click the Paste button. The *Qnifen* column instantly reappears to the left of the *Fiszol* column:

Suppose you decide to use the *Percent Change* column heading as the table's title. The first step is to insert a new row at the top of the table, like this:

1. Click an insertion point in cell A1, and choose Insert from the Table menu to display this dialog box:

Inserting rows

2. With Rows selected in the Insert group box and Before selected in the Placement group box, click OK to insert a new row at the top of the table. The cells have all been renumbered so that the first cell in the new row is cell A1.

Deleting columns or rows

To delete columns or rows from a table, select the column or row, and press the Delete key. In the Delete dialog box, confirm that you want to delete the column or row by clicking OK. (You can also erase the contents of the column or row without deleting the cells themselves.)

Moving cells

3. Now move the *Percent Change* heading. Click the top border of cell A2, and then use Cut and Paste or Drag And Drop Text (see page 34) to move the heading to cell A1.

Next, we must join the cells of the new row to create one large cell in order to accommodate the *Percent Change* heading. Joining cells is a simple two-step procedure:

Joining cells

1. Point to the top border of cell A1, hold down the left mouse button, and drag across row 1, releasing the mouse button when cells A1, B1, C1, and D1 are selected.

2. Right-click the selected cells, and choose Join Cells from the QuickMenu. The borders separating the columns in the first row disappear, creating one large cell.

Now finish the task by adding a column heading to cell A2:

1. Click cell A2, and type *Drug* as the new column heading. Here are the results:

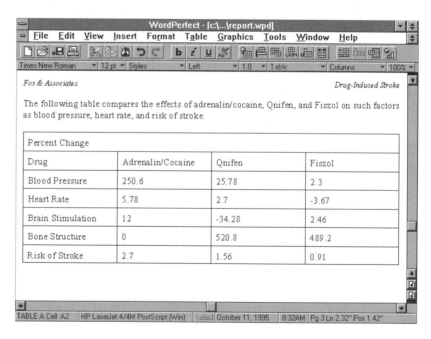

Jumping to a specific cell

To jump quickly to a specific location in a table, press Ctrl+G to display the Go To dialog box. You can specify a Position option that includes a variety of column, row, and cell references, such as Last Cell. Or you can enter a specific cell in a specific table, such as Table A and cell D4. When you click OK, WordPerfect takes you to the specified table and cell.

2. Click the Save button to save your work.

Changing Column Width and Row Height

You can adjust the width of any column and the height of any row to suit your needs. Follow these steps to change the widths of some of the columns in the sample table:

The Table Format button

1. With the insertion point still located in cell A2, click the Table Format button on the Toolbar to display this Format dialog box, and click the Column option at the top of the dialog box to display these settings:

2. In the Column Width group box, type *1.5* in the Width edit box, and click OK.

3. Now try adjusting columns with the mouse. Point to the border between cells C2 and D2, and when the pointer changes to a bar with opposing arrows, hold down the mouse button, and drag to the left. Release the mouse button when column C is about 1 inch wide. Repeat this procedure for column D. (To widen the columns, simply drag to the right.) The results are shown on the next page.

Adjusting with the mouse

Adjusting row height

By clicking the Row option in the Format dialog box, you can set the row height to accommodate one line or multiple lines of text. With the Single Line setting, text does not wrap within the cell and pressing Enter moves the insertion point to the next cell. With the Multi Line setting, text does wrap and pressing Enter moves the insertion point to the next line within the cell. You can also select automatic or fixed row height. With the Auto setting, WordPerfect adjusts the height based on the size of the text within the row. With the Fixed setting, you enter the height for each row.

Formatting Tables

Having made all the necessary structural changes to the table, let's add some formatting. We'll format the title and headings and align the number entries on the decimal point. Follow these steps:

1. Click an insertion point in cell A1, and click the Table Format button on the Toolbar to display the Format dialog

box. By default, WordPerfect displays these settings for the cell option:

2. In the Appearance group box, select Bold. Then select Large as the Size setting in the Text Size group box, and select Center as the Justification setting in the Alignment group box. Click OK to return to the document window.

3. Next, make all the headings in the *Drug* column bold. Drag down through cells A2 through A7, and click the Bold button on the Toolbar.

4. To center the headings in cells B2 through D2, select the three headings, click the Table Format button, select Center as the Justification setting, and click OK.

5. To decimal-align the numbers, drag through cells B3 through D7, and click the Table Format button. In the Format dialog box, select Decimal Align as the Justification setting, and click OK. The result is shown on the next page.

Table functions

WordPerfect provides a number of functions that make it possible to include complex calculations in your tables. Choose Formula Bar from the Table menu to display the Table Formula Feature Bar. You can enter formulas that perform calculations using values or cell references and the operators + (addition), - (subtraction), * (multiplication), and / (division). For example, you can add the entry in cell C4 to the entry in cell C6 by typing *C4+C6* in the formula edit box and clicking the Check Mark button. To quickly total the values in a range of cells, click an insertion point in a blank cell below the range, and click the Sum button on the Table Formula Bar. WordPerfect enters the total at the insertion point. You can perform more complex calculations using the functions listed in the Table Functions dialog box (click the Functions button to access this dialog box). Select a function from the list, and click the Insert button. WordPerfect inserts the function in the Formula edit box with placeholders for the information necessary to carry out the function. You then replace these placeholders with your own data. For example, average the entries in cells B3 through B7 by selecting the AVE(list) function and then replacing *list* with *B3:B7*. The cell entries in these examples must be numeric values, and you must first select the cell where you want the calculation results to appear. Experiment with formulas—you might come up with something like $E=mc^2$.

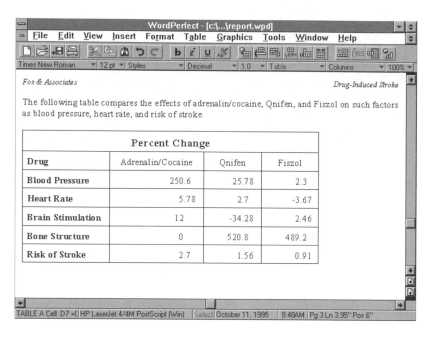

The following table compares the effects of adrenalin/cocaine, Qnifen, and Fiszol on such factors as blood pressure, heart rate, and risk of stroke.

Percent Change			
Drug	Adrenalin/Cocaine	Qnifen	Fiszol
Blood Pressure	250.6	25.78	2.3
Heart Rate	5.78	2.7	-3.67
Brain Stimulation	12	-34.28	2.46
Bone Structure	0	520.8	489.2
Risk of Stroke	2.7	1.56	0.91

6. The numbers still look a little ragged. To give them all the same number of decimal places, select the cells again (if necessary), and click the Number Type button on the Toolbar to display this dialog box:

The Number Type button

7. Select Fixed in the Available Types group box, and click OK. Here's the result:

Number types

WordPerfect's number types are fairly self-explanatory and will meet most of your needs. However, for those occasions when you need something special, you can create custom types. For example, to create a Currency type for British pounds, choose the Number Type command from the Table menu (or click the Number Type button on the Tables Toolbar), and select Currency in the Number Type dialog box. Next click the Custom button, change the Symbol setting to Pound (United Kingdom), and click OK twice. Now any number formatted as Currency will include the pound symbol.

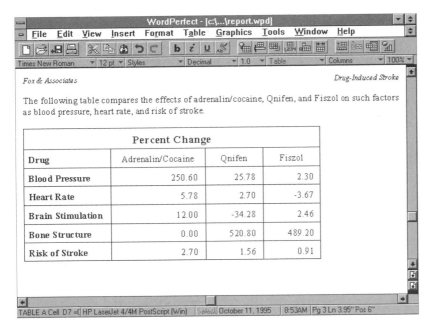

Next, let's change some of the lines in the table:

1. With the insertion point in cell A1, click the Lines/Fill button on the Toolbar to display this dialog box:

The Lines/Fill button

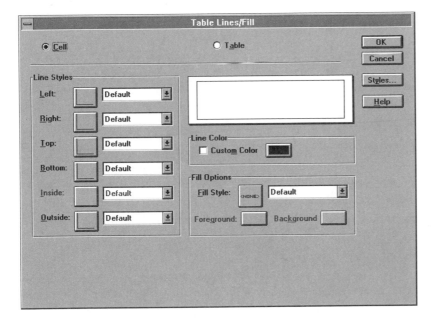

2. To change cell A1's bottom border, click the down arrow to the right of the Bottom option, and select Thick.

Adding a shadow to
the border

3. Click the Table option at the top of the dialog box to display these line and fill options, which apply to the entire table:

4. In the Border Lines group box, change the Border option to Shadow, and click OK.

The table is currently left-aligned, but it would look better centered. With WordPerfect, you don't have to worry about adjusting margins to center the table on the page. A couple of selections do the trick:

1. Be sure the insertion point is located in the table. Then click the Table Format button on the Toolbar, and in the Format dialog box, click the Table option to display the settings shown on the facing page.

Deleting tables

To delete an entire table from your document, point to one of the table's borders, and when the pointer changes to an arrow, triple-click to select the table. Then press the Delete key. In the Delete Table dialog box, you can tell WordPerfect to delete the entire table, the contents but not the structure, or the structure but not the contents. You can also specify that the table should be converted to a merge data file (see page 152).

2. In the Table Position group box, select Center, and then click OK to return to the document window, where the table has been centered between the left and right margins:

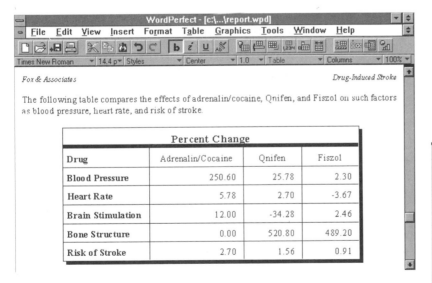

Importing Spreadsheets

WordPerfect's Table feature allows you to create impressive tables and perform a wide range of calculations with ease. But, suppose you have gone to a lot of trouble to create a spreadsheet of data in your favorite spreadsheet program and you now want to include that data in a report. It would be

Supported spreadsheet formats

Currently, files from the spreadsheet programs listed below can be imported into WordPerfect 6.1 for Windows documents:

PlanPerfect (3.0 through 5.1)
Lotus 1-2-3 (1A, 2.01, 2.3, 2.4, 3.0, and 3.1)
Excel (2.1, 3.0, and 4.0)
Quattro Pro for DOS (3.0 and 4.0)
Quattro Pro for Windows (1.0, 5.0, and 6.0)
Spreadsheet DIF

frustrating to have to rekey all that information into a Word-Perfect table for presentation. Fortunately, you don't have to. Using WordPerfect's Spreadsheet/Database command, you can import the spreadsheets you've spent hours slaving over directly into your WordPerfect documents.

To demonstrate, we'll pull a spreadsheet that we created with Quattro Pro 6.0 into the report. You can follow these steps with your own spreadsheet file:

1. Press Ctrl+End to move the insertion point below the table, press Enter twice, and choose Spreadsheet/Database and then Import from the Insert menu. This dialog box appears:

Creating links to spreadsheets

Instead of importing a spread-sheet into a WordPerfect document, you can link it, thereby maintaining a connection with the original data in the source program so that if the spreadsheet changes, the linked copy also changes. To link a spreadsheet, simply choose Spreadsheet/ Database and then Create Link from the Insert menu, and follow the procedure for importing a spreadsheet. In your document, WordPerfect displays the linked data as a table enclosed in non-printing link icons. You can edit the link and update the linked information at any time, and you can delete the link while retaining the spreadsheet data in its present form in your document.

2. In the Filename edit box, type the pathname of the spreadsheet you want to import (we typed *c:\office\qpw\profile.wb2*).

3. To import the spreadsheet as a WordPerfect table, accept the default Import As option, Table, by clicking OK. Word-Perfect enters a range of cells in the Range edit box.

4. If you don't want to import the specified range, type the range of cells that you want to import in the Range edit box, separating the first cell from the last cell in the range by two periods (we typed *A1..M7*).

5. Click OK. After a few seconds, you return to the document window, where the spreadsheet file has been imported as a table at the insertion point. You can then edit and format the

table in the document window. For example, we changed the font and size, decreased the width of the columns, and added a thick line and a shadow border to produce this result:

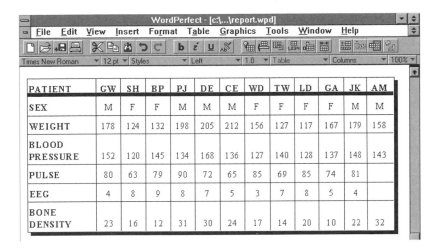

PATIENT	GW	SH	BP	PJ	DE	CE	WD	TW	LD	GA	JK	AM
SEX	M	F	F	M	M	M	F	F	F	F	M	M
WEIGHT	178	124	132	198	205	212	156	127	117	167	179	158
BLOOD PRESSURE	152	120	145	134	168	136	127	140	128	137	148	143
PULSE	80	63	79	90	72	65	85	69	85	74	81	
EEG	4	8	9	8	7	5	3	7	8	5	4	
BONE DENSITY	23	16	12	31	30	24	17	14	20	10	22	32

Creating Charts

WordPerfect allows you to turn tabular information into a chart without having to call on a spreadsheet or charting program for assistance. As a demonstration, we'll create a column chart based on the Quattro Pro spreadsheet we just imported, and then we'll add a little text for embellishment. If you haven't imported a spreadsheet, use the WordPerfect table we created at the beginning of the chapter so that you can see how easy it is to generate a chart in WordPerfect. Follow these steps:

1. Move the insertion point to the end of the report, just below the spreadsheet table, and press Enter.

2. In the table, select the cells containing the data you want to chart, including the row and column headings to be used as labels for the chart's axes and legend. Then click the Chart button on the Toolbar. WordPerfect Draw is activated (see the tip on page 143), the chart module opens, and the selected data is plotted in the three-dimensional bar chart format, as shown on the next page.

The Chart button

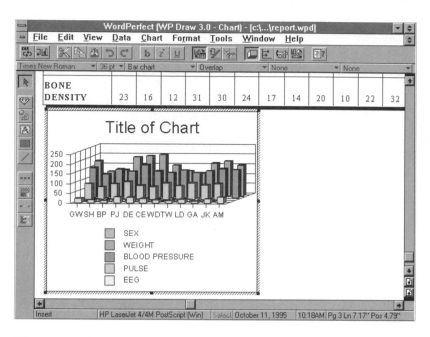

The menu bar, Toolbar, and Power Bar have all changed to provide you with the features you are most likely to use with charts. Because WordPerfect Draw has also been activated, a palette of drawing tools appears along the left side of the screen. Let's use some of these features to format the chart:

The 3D Chart button

1. Now click the 3D Chart button on the Toolbar to make the chart two-dimensional instead of three-dimensional.

The Layout button

2. Next click the Layout button on the Toolbar to display the Layout dialog box:

3. Select Cluster in the Style group box, change the Width setting in the Sizes group box to 100, and click OK.

The Horizontal Chart button

4. Click the Horizontal Chart button on the Toolbar to change the orientation of the chart. Here are the results:

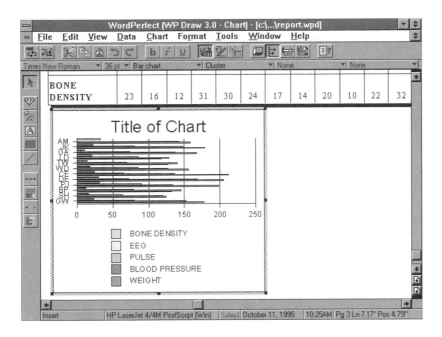

5. Now choose Titles from the Chart menu to display this dialog box:

Changing the title

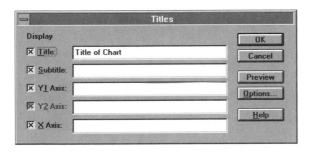

6. Type *Clinical Profile* in the Title edit box, and click OK.

7. Finally, choose Legend from the Chart menu to display this dialog box:

Using the Chart command

You can insert a chart in a Word-Perfect document without first selecting the chart data. Simply choose the Chart command from the Graphics menu. When the chart module opens, a datasheet and a sample chart appear. Using techniques similar to those for tables, you can then edit the "dummy" data in the datasheet, and the sample chart will automatically be updated. (To hide the datasheet, click the View Datasheet button on the Toolbar.) When you have finished, click outside the chart to return to the document window.

8. Change the Position option to Middle Right, and select the Vertical Orientation option. Select *Legend* in the Display Name edit box, and press the Delete key. Click the Series Font button, and in the Font dialog box, change the Font Size option to 14, and click OK. Then click OK to close the Legend dialog box.

Having set up the chart, let's return to the report and add some finishing touches:

1. Click anywhere outside the chart to return to the document window. (To once again open the chart module, simply double-click the chart.)

2. Align the chart with the right edge of the preceding table by dragging it with the mouse. Then click an insertion point, and add the explanatory text shown below to the left of the chart. Here are the results:

The chart module Power Bar

You can use the first two buttons on the chart module's Power Bar to change the font and font size of various chart elements, such as the title and legend text. The third button, Data Chart Types, offers a number of chart types to choose from. Using this button, you can change the default bar chart to a line or pie chart, for example. The Data Chart Style button offers a convenient way to alter the display of the data markers (the actual bars, lines, pie slices, and so on). For instance, you can cluster the data markers in groups or stack them one on top of the other. The last two buttons on the Power Bar allow you to place a border around a specific chart element, such as the title or legend.

Importing Graphics

Earlier in the chapter, you merged a spreadsheet into the report. The spreadsheet and report document were separate files that, after the merge, became one file. In a similar way, you can merge separate graphics files into your WordPerfect documents.

The WordPerfect 6.1 for Windows software package includes a number of ready-made graphics files that are suitable for many different types of documents. We'll use one of these files (MEDICAL1.WPG) to demonstrate how easy it is to import graphics with WordPerfect. You may want to speed things up a bit by turning off the Toolbar and Power Bar so that WordPerfect does not have to redraw these elements every time you return to the document window. (Choose their respective commands from the View menu.) Then follow these steps:

◄ **Ready-made graphics**

1. Press Ctrl+Home to move to the top of the report.

2. Choose Image from the Graphics menu to display the Insert Image dialog box:

3. Scroll to the MEDICAL1.WPG file, and double-click it. WordPerfect inserts the graphic at the top of the report's first page and displays the Graphics Box Feature Bar, as shown on the next page.

Supported graphics formats

In addition to WordPerfect's WPG format, you can import images in the following formats:

BMP	PCX
CGM	PIC
DRW	PCT
DXF	TGA
EPS	TIF
HPG	WMF

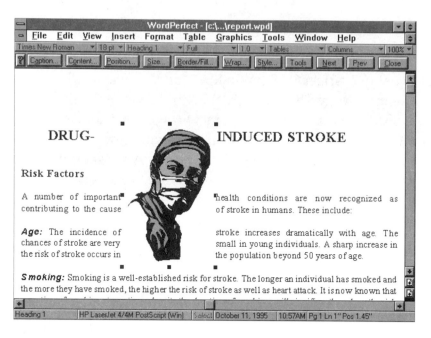

No wisecracks about Dr. Bob! He serves as a good example, and besides, he makes house calls.

Editing Graphics

After you import the graphic, you can change its size, position, and so on to suit your needs. Let's turn the graphic into a small logo:

Adjusting the size

1. If necessary, click the graphic to select it. Then move the mouse pointer over the handle in the bottom-left corner of the graphics box. When the pointer changes to a double-headed arrow, hold down the left mouse button, and drag up and to the right to decrease the size of the graphics box. When you release the mouse button, the graphic also decreases in size.

Adjusting the position

2. Move the mouse pointer inside the selected graphics box, and when the pointer changes to a four-headed arrow, hold down the left mouse button, and drag the graphic's "placeholder" (the box with the dashed lines) to the top-left corner of the report. When you release the mouse button, the graphic moves into position, like this:

Notice that the text of the report wraps around the graphic. You can adjust the text flow in a variety of ways. We'll do that next, and at the same time, we'll fine-tune the position and size of the graphics box, customize its borders, and add a caption. Follow these steps:

1. Be sure the graphic is still selected. Then on the Graphics Box Bar, click Wrap to display the Wrap Text dialog box:

2. Because the graphic is supposed to be a logo, we don't want the text of the report to flow around it, so in the Wrapping Type group box, select Neither Side, and click OK. (Don't worry if the appearance of the title changes; we'll fix that later.)

3. Next, click the Position button on the Graphics Box Bar to display the dialog box shown on the next page.

WordPerfect Draw

WordPerfect comes with a sophisticated drawing program called WordPerfect Draw (WP Draw). You can use WP Draw to manipulate graphics from other sources and to create your own graphics. To activate WP Draw, choose the Draw command from the Graphics menu. WP Draw inserts a drawing area in the current document and displays a palette of drawing tools. As well as drawing straight and curved lines, you can draw freeform objects, circles, ellipses, squares, rectangles, and polygons, and these shapes can be hollow or filled. You can vary the color and style of both the lines and the fill pattern. You can add text in the usual range of fonts and sizes, and you can apply a wide variety of attributes. If you want to get fancy, you can rotate a graphic by choosing Rotate from the Edit menu and then dragging one of the handles in the desired direction. You can even choose Flip Left/Right or Flip Top/Bottom from the Graphics menu to have your graphic do an about-face or stand on its head. When you're finished drawing, click outside the drawing area to return to your document.

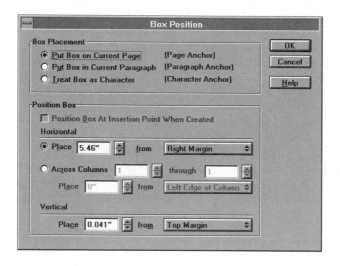

4. To fix the position of the graphic on the page, check that the Put Box On Current Page option is selected. Then change the Horizontal Place setting to *1* inch from Left Edge Of Page, change the Vertical Place setting to *0.5* inch from Top Of Page, and click OK.

5. Click the Size button on the Graphics Box Bar to display this dialog box:

6. Change the Width and Height settings to *1* inch, and click OK.

Adding a shadow

7. Click the Border/Fill button on the Graphics Box Bar to display the Box Border/Fill Styles dialog box (which is similar to the dialog box on page 62). Select the Shadow Border Style option, and click the Customize Style button to display this dialog box:

8. In the Drop Shadow group box, click Type, and select the second shadow style. In the Corners group box, change the Radius setting to *1*. WordPerfect displays a sample border with your selections in place. If you like this effect, click OK twice to return to the document window.

Now we can create the caption for the graphic:

1. Click the Caption button on the Graphics Box Bar to display this dialog box:

← Adding a caption

2. Accept all the default settings, and click the Edit button.

3. Back in the document window, press the Backspace key to delete *Figure 1*, and then type *The Fox Report*. Select the caption, choose Font from the Format menu, click Italic, set the Relative Size option to Small, and click OK. Then choose Justification and Center from the Format menu.

4. Click anywhere in the document, and click the Close button on the Graphics Box Bar.

5. If necessary, click an insertion point in the title of the report, display the Power Bar, select <None> from the Select Style drop-down list, and then select Heading 1 from the Select Style list to reapply that style. Then save your changes. The logo now looks like this:

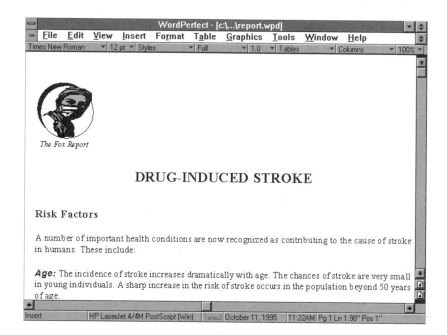

Printing Specific Pages

So far, printing your documents has been pretty straightforward. If you've been working with the sample report, you now have a longer document on your screen that we can use to explore another printing option. Follow these steps:

1. First check the page breaks in Two Page view by choosing Two Page from the View menu. The first two pages of the report should look something like this:

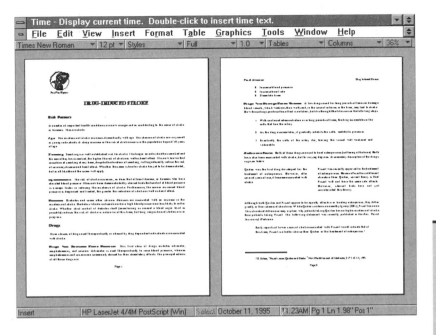

2. Press PgDn a couple of times to check the layout of pages 2 and 3.

3. If everything looks beautiful, choose Print from the File menu to display the Print dialog box. In the Print Selection group box, you can select Full Document to print the entire document, Current Page to print only the page on which the insertion point is currently located, or Multiple Pages to print more than one page.

4. Select the Multiple Pages option, and then click the Print button to display the Multiple Pages dialog box:

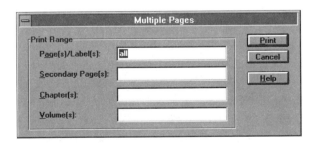

5. In the Page(s)/Label(s) edit box, type *1*, a space, then *3*, and click Print to print the first and third pages of the report. (To print the second and third pages, you would enter *2-3*.) Your printer responds by producing the pages on which you have placed graphics so that you can admire your work.

Other printing options

If you've set up secondary pages, chapters, or volumes in the Page Numbering dialog box (see the tip on page 121), you can print the specific pages assigned to those components of your document by specifying the pages in the Multiple Pages dialog box. You can access other printing options by clicking the Options button in the Print dialog box. For example, you can print only the odd and only the even pages (to facilitate copying on both sides of the page when you don't have a copier with a duplex option), and you can print in reverse order (also to facilitate copying on certain types of copiers). If you have created a document summary (see page 76), you can print it by selecting the Print Document Summary option. If you have subdivided your pages (by choosing Page and then Subdivide Page from the Format menu) and formatted the pages appropriately, you can select Booklet Printing to have Word-Perfect print more than one document page on each sheet of paper in such a way that you can fold the paper to create a booklet.

7

Time-Saving Form Documents: Merging Letters and Labels

Create form letters for mass mailings using a customer data file

David Robertson
Sullivan, Duffy and Bridge, Attorneys at Law
145 Salmon Street
Portland, OR 97201

Dear Dave,

I am writing to inform you th
and phone number of our nev

Fox & Associates
Medical Malpractice Consult
1022 SW Vermont Street
Portland, OR 97223
(503) 555-6789

We look forward to continu
Attorneys at Law. Please feel

Thank you,

Kaye E. Fox, Ph.D.

Ms. Alannah Burke
Burke-Roney Law Offices
246 NE 42nd
Seattle, WA 98117

Dear Alannah,

I am writing to inform you that we will be moving to a new location on November 1. The address and phone number of our new offices will be:

Fox & Associates
Medical Malpractice Consultants
1022 SW Vermont Street
Portland, OR 97223
(503) 555-6789

We look forward to continuing to provide consulting services to Burke-Roney Law Offices. Please feel free to contact us at any time during our regular office hours.

Thank you,

Kaye E. Fox, Ph.D.

Fox & Associates
Medical Malpractice Consultants
1224 Evergreen Road
Lake Oswego, OR 97035

David Robertson
Sullivan, Duffy and Bridge, Attorneys at Law
145 Salmon Street
Portland, OR 97201

Let WordPerfect take care of positioning the return address

Create letters and envelopes in the same merge operation

If you need to send the same letter to half a dozen of your clients, you can create a template letter and quickly fill in the name, address, and salutation for each client. But what if you need to send the letter to a hundred clients? And what if you communicate regularly with the same set of clients? Isn't there a way to avoid having to type those names and addresses over and over again?

The time-saver you're looking for is WordPerfect's Merge feature. You can use Merge to create "personalized" letters and envelopes for mass mailings, as well as a whole host of other documents, such as phone lists, invoices, memos, and contracts. To use the Merge feature properly, you need to be familiar with some jargon, so we'll start with a few definitions, using a form letter as an example. To create a form letter, you need to create a *form file* and a *data file*. Let's talk about the data file first.

The data file

The *data file* contains the information that changes from letter to letter, such as the names and addresses of the recipients. Collectively, the information that will be merged into one letter—in our example, a name, company name, address, and salutation—is referred to as a *record*, and each item within one record is referred to as a *field*. To understand this relationship, take a look at this data file:

Records and fields

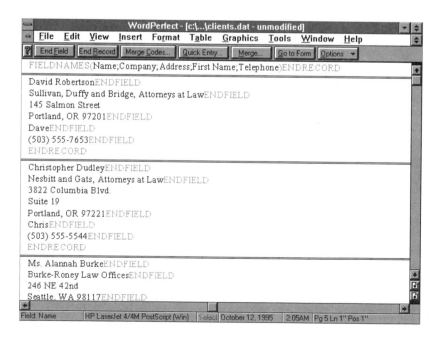

The records are separated by ENDRECORD codes, followed by hard page breaks. The fields within each record are separated by ENDFIELD codes followed by hard returns.

You can include as many records as you want (or as many as disk space permits) in a data file, and you can include as many as 255 fields in each record. However, every record must contain the same number of fields, and every field must either contain the same type of information or be empty. For example, field 5 of every record in the example contains a telephone number. If you have a record with no phone number, field 5 of that record remains empty but still ends with an ENDFIELD code and a hard return.

The *form file* contains the information that does not change from letter to letter—the text of the letter. This file also controls the merging process by means of codes that you insert as placeholders for the information that does change from letter to letter. Here's an example:

The form file

The FIELD(Name) merge code is a placeholder for the information contained in the Name field in the records of the data file, the FIELD(Company) merge code is a placeholder for the information in the Company field, and so on.

Creating Form Letters

Let's create the sample data and form files so that you can see how merging works. Because you will probably use the same data file with more than one form file, you'll usually start by creating the data file, which in this case is a "database" of clients' names, addresses, and telephone numbers. (The telephone numbers aren't used in the example, but they might be needed with other form files.)

Creating the Data File

Each record in the data file we're going to create contains five fields: names in the first, company names in the second, addresses in the third, first names in the fourth, and phone numbers in the fifth. Fields do not have to contain the same number of characters or even the same number of lines. For example, the Address field in the second record might contain an address that is three lines long, whereas the Address field in the third record might contain an address that is only two lines long.

Starting with a clear screen and the Toolbar and the Power Bar hidden, follow these steps to create the data file, using the sample names and addresses or your own:

Starting the merge process → 1. Choose the Merge command from the Tools menu to display this dialog box:

2. Click the Data button to display this dialog box:

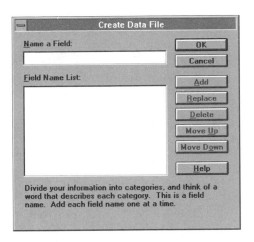

3. In the Name A Field edit box, type *Name*, and then click Add or press Enter to add the first field to the Field Name List box.

4. Now type *Company* in the Name A Field edit box, and click Add or press Enter to add the second field to the Field Name List box. Then do the same for the *Address*, *First Name*, and *Telephone* fields. (If you make a mistake while entering a field name in the Create Data File dialog box, select the field name in the Field Name List box, and then select the appropriate option to replace, delete, or reposition the field name.)

5. Click OK to display this dialog box:

The Quick Data Entry dialog box greatly simplifies the task of constructing the data file's records. (Notice that the five

Editing the data file

You can edit a data file in the Quick Data Entry dialog box. To display the Quick Data Entry dialog box, click the Quick Entry button on the Merge Feature Bar. Then use the options at the bottom of the dialog box to switch between the first, previous, next, and last records in the data file. To delete the current record, click Delete Record. You can search for a particular record by clicking Find and entering search text in the Find Text dialog box. (Use the options at the top of the dialog box to broaden or narrow your search.) Select the Field Names option to edit, add, or delete field names. When you have finished, click Close. You can also edit a data file directly in the document window using the Merge Feature Bar. Make changes to the records as you would normally, including ENDFIELD and ENDRECORD codes where necessary by clicking the End Field and End Record buttons on the Merge Feature Bar.

fields you just created are all present and accounted for.) Follow these steps:

1. In the Name edit box, type *David Robertson*, and then press Tab to move to the Company edit box.

2. Type *Sullivan, Duffy and Bridge, Attorneys at Law*, and press Tab to move to the Address edit box.

Fields with more than one line of text →

3. Type the following address in the Address edit box, pressing Ctrl+Enter rather than Enter to start the second line of the address. If the first line disappears while you're typing the second one, don't worry. WordPerfect has just tucked it out of the way for the time being. (To see the first line of the address, click the up arrow at the end of the Address edit box.)

145 Salmon Street
Portland, OR 97201

4. In the First Name edit box, type *Dave*, and in the Telephone edit box, type *(503) 555-7653*.

5. To start a new record, simply click the New Record button, and then enter the two records below. (Remember to press Ctrl+Enter to start a new line in the same field.)

Christopher Dudley
Nesbitt and Gats, Attorneys at Law
3822 Columbia Blvd. (press Ctrl+Enter)
Suite 19 (press Ctrl+Enter)
Portland, OR 97221
Chris
(503) 555-5544

Ms. Alannah Burke
Burke-Roney Law Offices
246 NE 42nd (press Ctrl+Enter)
Seattle, WA 98117
Alannah
(206) 555-9901

Data tables

If you prefer to use a table as your data file, choose Merge from the Tools menu, select the Place Records In A Table option, and click Data. Then enter the field names (or numbers, if you prefer) in the Create Data File dialog box, and click OK. You can have up to 64 fields, or columns, in a data table. When the Quick Data Entry dialog box appears, fill in the records as you would for a data text file, and then click Close to create the table. You can edit a data table using the Quick Data Entry dialog box as explained in the tip on page 153. You can also edit the data table directly in the document window using the Merge Feature Bar. For example, to add rows (records) or columns (fields), be sure the insertion point is positioned inside the table, and then click the Row or Column button to add or delete a row or column.

6. After you finish creating the three records of your data file, click Close in the Quick Data Entry dialog box.

7. When WordPerfect asks whether you want to save your changes, click Yes and save the file with the name *clients*. (WordPerfect automatically appends the DAT extension.) When you return to the document window, notice that the Merge Feature Bar has dropped into place below the menu bar. Your data file should now look like the one on page 149.

Creating the Form File

Now we're ready to create a form file that makes use of the data file's name and address database. Follow these steps:

1. Click the Merge button on the Merge Bar, and then click the Form button in the Merge dialog box.

2. When the Create Merge File dialog box appears, be sure the New Document Window option is selected, and click OK. WordPerfect displays this dialog box:

3. To associate the CLIENTS.DAT data file with the new form file, be sure the Associate A Data File option is selected, and then click the small button with the folder icon to the right of the edit box to display the Select File dialog box shown on the next page.

Sorting records

You can use WordPerfect's Sort feature to sort records in your data files. Simply choose Sort from the Tools menu (or click the Options button on the Merge Feature Bar and select Sort), enter the input and output files, if necessary, and then select from the Defined Sorts list box or click the New button to define a custom sort. (You can also edit a defined Sort by clicking the Edit button.) When you click the New button, WordPerfect displays the New Sort dialog box, where you can specify the field to sort on, the type of sort (alphabetic or numeric), and the sort order (ascending or descending). If you want to sort on a specific field, or if you want to sort on more than one field, use the options in the Key Definitions group box. For example, to sort on the second and then third fields in a data file, enter *2* in the first field box, click the Add Key option to add another key definition, and enter *3* in the next field box. You can click the Insert Key option to add another key definition above the current definition or the Delete Key option to delete the current definition. You can also use operators, such as |, &, =, <, and >, to select specific records with or without sorting the records.

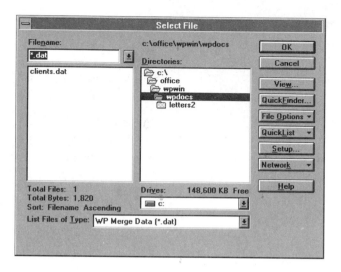

Adding dates and prompts

You can add the current date to a form file by inserting a DATE code. Simply position the insertion point where you want the date to appear, and click the Date button on the Merge Feature Bar. You can also add a KEYBOARD merge code to a form file so that a prompt requesting additional input from the user is displayed when the merge is performed. To insert a KEYBOARD merge code, position the insertion point in the form file where you want the prompt to appear, click the Keyboard button on the Merge Feature Bar, type a prompt such as *Enter special remarks here*, and then click OK. When you merge the form file with a data file, WordPerfect pauses at each record and displays the prompt so that you can enter additional information. (While the keyboard merge is in progress, you can use the buttons on the Merge Feature Bar to continue on to the next record, skip the current record, and so on.)

4. Double-click CLIENTS.DAT, and then back at the Create Form File dialog box, click OK.

Now follow these steps to enter the text of the form letter:

1. Press Enter twice, and type the following:

I am writing to inform you that we will be moving to a new location on November 1. The address and phone number of our new offices will be:

Fox & Associates
Medical Malpractice Consultants
1022 SW Vermont Street
Portland, OR 97223
(503) 555-6789

We look forward to continuing to provide consulting services for your firm. Please feel free to contact us at any time during our regular office hours.

Thank you,

Kaye E. Fox, Ph.D.

2. Press Ctrl+Home to move to the top of the letter where you will insert the placeholder merge codes, and click the Insert Field button on the Merge Bar to display this dialog box:

3. With Name selected, click Insert to insert the FIELD(Name) merge code, and press Enter to start a new line. The dialog box stays open so that you can continue entering merge codes.

4. Select Company, click Insert to insert a FIELD(Company) merge code, press Enter to start a new line, select Address, click Insert to insert a FIELD(Address) merge code, and press Enter twice.

5. Type *Dear* followed by a space, and without moving the insertion point, select the First Name field, and click Insert to insert a FIELD(First Name) merge code after the word *Dear*.

6. Click Close to close the dialog box, and type a comma after the FIELD(First Name) merge code. Your form file now looks like the one on page 149.

7. You can use a field more than once in a form file. For example, delete the words *your firm* from the second paragraph, click the Insert Field button, insert a FIELD(Company) merge code, and close the dialog box. The form file now looks like this one:

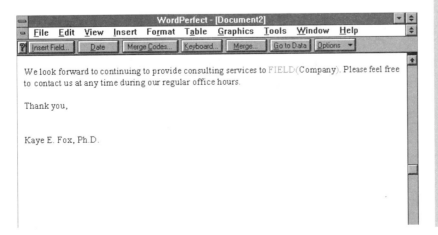

Using a field more than once

Merge options

Use the Options button on the Merge Feature Bar to sort and print data files and to display, disguise (as markers), or hide merge codes. You can also tailor your merge by clicking Options in the Perform Merge dialog box. Then, when the Perform Merge Options dialog box is displayed, select the desired options, such as whether to separate the merged documents with page breaks, the number of copies for each record, and whether to leave a blank line for empty fields.

Bar codes

You can add POSTNET (Postal Numeric Encoding Technique) bar codes to your envelopes to improve delivery accuracy and reduce postage costs. POSTNET bar codes can be regular five-digit or nine-digit ZIP codes, or they can be eleven-digit DPBCs (Delivery Point Bar Codes). A DPBC consists of a nine-digit ZIP code plus the last two digits of a residence or business number, such as *Kaye E. Fox, Medical Malpractice Consultants, 1224 Evergreen Road, Lake Oswego, OR 97035-5678-24*. To add a bar code to an envelope, choose Envelope from the Format menu, click Options in the Envelope dialog box, select one of the Include USPS Bar Code options, and click OK. Back in the Envelope dialog box, click an insertion point in the POSTNET Bar Code edit box in the Mailing Addresses group box so that you can enter the ZIP or DPBC code. (If the Mailing Addresses box already contains an address, WordPerfect automatically enters the ZIP code in the POST-NET Bar Code edit box. If you're using a DPBC code, you must still enter the two additional digits.) WordPerfect converts the code to a series of tall and short lines. To add bar codes to regular text, choose Other and then Bar Code from the Insert menu. When the POSTNET Bar Code dialog box appears, enter the bar code digits, and click OK. (This can be handy for envelopes with "see-through" windows.)

8. Choose Close from the File menu, and save the form file with the name *move*. (WordPerfect automatically appends the FRM extension.)

Merging and Printing Letters and Envelopes

This is the moment of truth. If you have inserted the codes correctly, merging the form and data files will be a piece of cake. And you can create envelopes while you're at it! Follow these steps:

1. Click the Merge button on the Merge Bar, and then click the Merge option to display this dialog box:

2. Because the data file is still open, WordPerfect has entered its path and filename in the Data File edit box. The form file is closed, so click the arrow at the end of the Form File edit box, click Select File, and when the Select Form File dialog box appears, double-click MOVE.FRM.

3. Click the Envelopes button, and enter the information below in the Return Addresses box of the Envelope dialog box:

Fox & Associates
Medical Malpractice Consultants
1224 Evergreen Road
Lake Oswego, OR 97035

4. Because you want to use the data file addresses, you need to add merge codes to the Mailing Addresses box, just as you did in the form file. Click the Mailing Addresses box, and then click the Field button at the bottom of the dialog box to display the Insert Field Name Or Number dialog box. Select the Name field, click Insert, and press Enter to start a new line. Do the same for the Company and Address fields. The Envelope dialog box should now look like this:

5. Click OK, and in the Perform Merge dialog box, click OK again to begin the merging operation. (You can press Esc or Ctrl+Break at any time to cancel the merge.)

When the merging operation is complete, WordPerfect has created a new document containing the merged letters separated by page breaks, followed by the merged envelopes. Let's take a look:

1. Press Ctrl+Home to move to the top of the first letter:

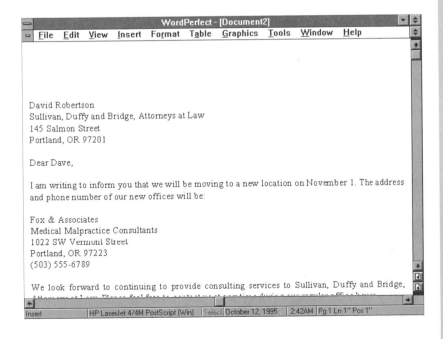

Selective merging

Use the Select Records option at the bottom of the Perform Merge dialog box to select specific records from the data file to merge with the form file. You can then specify certain conditions that the records must meet or mark the records that you want to include in the merge. If you select Specify Conditions, click the Example button on the right side of the Select Records dialog box to see examples of how to enter conditions. If you select Mark Records, WordPerfect presents you with a list of the records in the current data file. To select specific records, simply click the small box to the left of each record in the Record List box. You can change the way records are redisplayed in this list by selecting options in the Records To Mark group box. For example, change the range of records displayed by clicking the arrows next to the Display Records From and To boxes and then clicking the Update Record List button. To change the display of fields in the Record List box, select a field from the First Field To Display drop-down list, and then click the Update Record List button. Use the Mark All Records In List or Unmark All Records In List buttons to select or deselect all the records in the Record List box.

2. Scroll down through the other letters. As you can see, Word-Perfect replaced the merge codes in the form file with the names and addresses from the data file to create a "personalized" letter for each record.

3. Now scroll down to the first envelope, choose Zoom from the View menu, select 50%, and click OK to get an idea of how the printed envelopes will look:

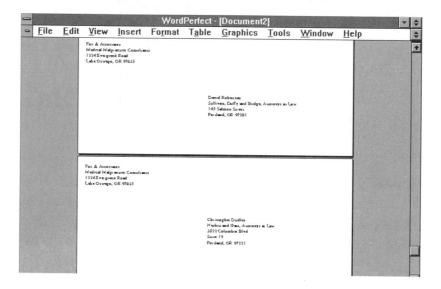

4. Use the Zoom command to return to 100% Page view. Then choose Save As command from the File menu, and save the merged file with the name *lettmrg*.

Independent envelopes

Keep in mind that you can create envelopes independently of the merge procedure by using the Envelope command on the Format menu.

Now let's print the merged letters and envelopes. (If your printer does not have an envelope feed and cannot print in landscape mode—perpendicular to the inserted edge of the envelope—you might not be able to print envelopes.)

1. Press Ctrl+Home to move to the top of the first letter, and choose Print from the File menu. Because the letters and envelopes are separated by hard page breaks, they print on separate pages. (Be prepared to manually feed envelopes and make any settings required by your printer.)

Canceling printing

To cancel the printing of merged documents (or any document), choose the Print command from the File menu, click the Control button, and in the WordPerfect Print Job dialog box, click Cancel Print Job.

2. Choose Close from the File menu to close LETTMRG.WPD.

Creating Labels

We mentioned earlier that you will often use a data file with more than one form file. To use the CLIENTS.DAT data file with a form file that produces labels, try this:

1. Choose New from the File menu, and click Select to open a new blank document, and then choose Labels from the Format menu to display this dialog box:

2. WordPerfect enables you to set up labels to print on many types of commercially available label sheets. Scroll through the list of available label formats until you find one that suits your needs. WordPerfect displays the size of the highlighted label format in the Label Details box. A label sample is also displayed in the bottom-right corner of the dialog box.

Selecting a label format

3. With the desired label format highlighted, click Select. (We selected Avery 5260 because our printer can easily handle these sheets of thirty 2.63-inch-by-1-inch labels.) Word-Perfect returns you to the document window, where a label is represented as a white box on a gray background.

Now all you have to do is add merge codes to the blank label so that it can be merged with the CLIENTS.DAT data file:

1. Choose Merge from the Tools menu, and then click the Form button in the Merge dialog box.

2. When the Create Merge File dialog box appears, be sure the Use File In Active Window option is selected, and click OK.

3. In the Create Form File dialog box, click the small button with the folder icon to display the Select File dialog box. Double-click CLIENTS.DAT to associate the data file with the new form file, and then click OK to return to the document window, where the Merge Bar is displayed.

4. With the insertion point at the top of the label, click the Insert Field button on the Merge Bar. Be sure Name is selected in the Insert Field Name Or Number dialog box, click Insert, and press Enter to start a new line. Then insert Company and press Enter. Finally, insert Address, but this time don't press Enter.

5. Click Close to close the dialog box. Here's the result:

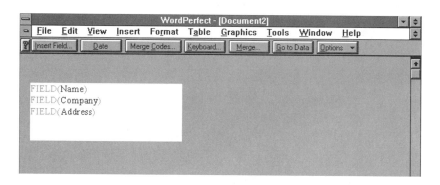

6. Choose Save As from the File menu, and save the label form file as *labels*.

Before we actually merge the LABELS.FRM form file with the CLIENTS.DAT data file, let's add a little formatting. (You can format the labels after the merge, but it's much more efficient to make those changes in the form file.) Follow these steps:

Creating phone lists

You can use the information from a data file, like the one on page 149, to generate a phone list. All you have to do is create a form file with a merge code for the Name field from the data file. Then set a tab around the 3- or 4-inch position, and insert a merge code for the Telephone field from the data file. Finally, press Enter to move the insertion point below the FIELD(Name) merge code, click the Merge Codes button on the Merge Feature Bar, and select PAGEOFF from the Insert Merge Codes dialog box. (The PAGEOFF code will turn off the hard page breaks that WordPerfect includes in the data file.) Save the new form file, and perform the merge.

1. Move the insertion point to the top of the label, choose Font from the Format menu, and then select a smaller font size, such as 10.

Formatting the labels

2. Next choose Typesetting and then Advance from the Format menu, and in the Advance dialog box, select the Down From Insertion Point option, type *0.1* in the Vertical Distance edit box, and click OK to create a little space at the top of the label.

Now let's do some merging:

1. Click the Merge button on the Merge Bar, and then click the Merge option.

Merging the labels

2. In the Perform Merge dialog box, check that *<Current Document>* appears in the Form File edit box and that the correct pathname for CLIENTS.DAT appears in the Data File edit box. Click the Reset button to change *All Records; Envelope* to just *All Records*, and then click OK.

3. Zoom to 75% to see these results:

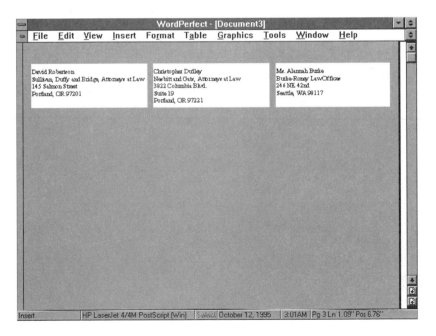

4. Save the merged labels as *labelmrg*, and if you happen to have a sheet of the specified label format handy (in this case, Avery 5260), load the sheet into your printer's paper tray and print the labels.

Printing the labels

Index